In The Morning Light

by Patricia Robbins

2nd Tier Publishing

Published by:
   2nd Tier Publishing
   501 Wimberley Oaks Dr
   Wimberley, TX 78676-4671, U.S.A.

Source of quotes: The documentary "Which Doctor", produced by Matthew
and Debra Mitchell; a Channel 2 News program from San Francisco, featuring
Charlotte and Vanessa and The Center for Attitudinal Healing; and from their
journals and mine.

ISBN 978-0-578-10813-1

Book design by Dan Gauthier, 2nd Tier Publishing

Dedication

To Charlotte and Vanessa for all the love and joy we shared in this life that now resides deep in my heart. You taught your dad and me what courage is and how to be thankful for each and every day.

To Jeff, my husband, lover and friend, for his strength, wisdom and enduring love.

Acknowledgments

I am eternally grateful to all of my friends and family who were there to help in so many ways, bringing comfort, joy and laughter to our lives. We would never have made it without you.

To Dan Gauthier and Shiila Safer, 2nd Tier Publishing, your creative spirit, compassion and dedication to detail transformed this manuscript into my dream, a published book.

Sally Arteseros, my editor, for making my story flow and for her thoughtful guidance.

The Ucross Foundation, Ucross Wyoming for generously granting me a six-week residency to journey into writing without interruption while enjoying the natural beauty of Wyoming.

All the doctors, nurses, respiratory therapists, medical technicians, volunteers at The Center for Attitudinal Healing, and art therapists who cared for the girls over so many years with such love and devotion.

Chapter 1

Charlotte, Pat, Vanessa

"There's rosemary, that's for remembrance; pray, love, remember."

"Hamlet" by Shakespeare

I am a mother. I was a mother. I am no longer a mother. Ten months ago my daughter Charlotte died of cystic fibrosis and four months later her identical twin sister Vanessa followed. Never in my life had I taken their breath for granted.

In the morning, I am leaving my home in Pennsylvania for California, hoping to muster up the courage to begin sorting through the remaining remnants of their lives; remembering how they had carefully chosen each little treasure when they packed up their childhood memories to begin life anew in the land of dreams.

All night, a cool breeze drifts through our bedroom window, as I lie awake watching the curtains billow in such a way, they seem to be breathing. I snuggle down deep for warmth under the covers while trying to fall asleep, but my mind will not let go.

The fear of leaving the safety of my home, the comfort of my routine, the sheltered cocoon constructed to protect myself in my grieving, stays with me. Am I ready to venture out into the world of reality?

Over and over, through the night, I slip silently from our bed, trying not to wake my husband, wandering room to room, feeling lost in the empty spaces, hearing the echoes of the girls' voices, their laughter, trying to swallow the impending scream in the back of my throat. Afraid, if released, it will never stop.

Each time slipping back into bed, I nestle over to capture the warmth of Jeff's body, fitting so well into the soft, smooth, curve of his back, hoping to hold him close enough so that somehow, some way, my body will melt into his and I can lose this attempt at living without a spark of life left inside of me.

But as the night passes, and the soft morning light filters through the open window, I realize no one can strip this emptiness from me and I will be on that morning flight. Driving to the airport in silence, Jeff and I say our good-byes and I numbly board the plane.

❧

Stepping off the aircraft onto California soil, I'm confused and a bit sick to my stomach. For more than three years, countless times I've made the trip from Philadelphia to San Francisco in a panic, thinking I wouldn't make it in time to find my daughters alive. But always I did make it. Now I'm back, without the panic, without the urgency, without the girls.

I run and catch the Marin Airporter shuttle bus to make the familiar journey across the Golden Gate Bridge to my sister's home in Tiburon. As the bus winds its way down Nineteenth Avenue, passing through Golden Gate Park, the familiar spicy scent of eucalyptus fills the air and my mind drifts back.

❧

September 1970. My husband Jeff and I meet in a communications class at Trenton State College in New Jersey. I was, as Jeff would later recall, wearing my "brother's brown tie shoes" and a thin, braided, leather band encircling my neck, a gift from my current boyfriend. My hair was waist long, nut brown. Jeff, with his reticent smile, wild ebony hair, and a gentleness I had never before encountered in a man, had recently been discharged from the army, serving as a medic in a field hospital in Nha Trang, Vietnam. Somehow, he seemed older than his twenty-four years.

We had an assignment to see the movie Z, and since he knew the area, he suggested we go together. Working as a waitress during the day while going to school at night, I recently had moved into an apartment with my friend Eileen. Jeff was living at his parents' home, farming during the day and like me, going to school full time at night. We became fast friends.

Most days if we weren't working or going to school, we were usually together at my apartment. On weekends, even if I went to visit my boyfriend at Rutgers University, Jeff would sometimes come over to work on assignments from our drawing and painting classes. My roommate Eileen loved the company and we were all so comfortable together, it worked.

About a month after we met, on a sparkling clear Saturday in October, the kind you long for in the heat of summer, Jeff and I drove over to Bowman's Tower in Bucks County, Pennsylvania for a picnic. We ate our lunch atop a meandering stone wall and afterwards took a long walk around the park, stopping under a big oak tree to rest and shade ourselves from the sun. The air was crisp with the anticipation of winter, but the sun was warm as it filtered through the branches of trees, creating small patches of heat on the skin of our bare arms.

We spread our blanket and lay down next to each other, facing the sky. Jeff turned, propped himself up on his elbow and leaned his body so close I could feel the warmth of his skin glance across my arm. "Look straight above, past the trees and watch the clouds as they pass through the leaves. You'll see the sky in a whole different way."

As I lay on my back watching the sky seem to pass through a vast array of ruby red, sunflower yellow, poppy orange and rust-rotted sienna colored leaves, my admiration for Jeff grew. He noticed the little things in life and took the time to enjoy them. I liked that.

The following month, passion was intertwined with our friendship. We were in my apartment one night after communications class, lying on the living room floor, listening to music. Jeff reached over, placed his hand over mine, and gently stroked each of my fingers, one at a time. A feeling of warmth radiated from his touch, shivered through my body and awakened me as if I had been asleep. We spent the night in each other's arms, enjoying the intimacy of our bodies and minds. After that night, we were rarely apart.

When classes ended that spring, we decided to do some traveling. At the end of the summer, we collected our paychecks, loaded up our possessions and headed west on the Pennsylvania Turnpike.

We lived and went to school for a time in the Southwest and California before deciding to get serious about our education and transferred our credits to the University of Missouri for our sophomore year. They had a veterinary school for Jeff and a respected anthropology department for me.

This turned out to be a wonderful decision for both of us. We relished being back in school and immersed ourselves in study. For fun, we watched movies several nights a week on campus, and on weekends walked for hours exploring the parks, rivers and small towns in the area. We both had a love nature and this just brought us closer.

At the end of my sophomore year, I decided to study and collaborate on some research with my anthropology professor in Sweden the following year. Jeff, my constant cheerleader, encouraged me and helped make it happen.

The reality of actually leaving one another for a year was another story and it didn't hit me until we were actually saying good-bye at the airport gate. For the past three years we had rarely been apart and now I wondered: would our love survive this long separation?

After six weeks of intensive language classes in Hudiksvall, in northern Sweden, I journeyed for two days by train to Fellingsbro, a small town in central Sweden, two hours west of Stockholm, to the school that would be my home for the coming year.

At the welcome party that evening, standing in a room full of strangers speaking only Swedish, I had never felt so alone in my life. Little did I realize at the time that this would be the beginning of my journey into becoming more independent and finding the strength and resources within me to cope in this world, something I would certainly need for my life to come.

After a week of classes, much to the chagrin of my anthropology professor, I chanced upon the weaving room at school and fell into its magic. Amidst all the protests, my plans changed for the year and weaving became my passion. In the community I joined local spinning and dyeing groups, soaking up both their knowledge and their friendship. Working with my hands provided a deep satisfaction within me and since the creative process permeates all aspects of Swedish life, I relished it.

Over time, my loneliness diminished, while my affection for Jeff grew through the letters we wrote every day to one another. In 1973, there was no easy or inexpensive way to stay in touch except through the mail, which meant two weeks for an answer to a question, one week over and one week back.

But I saw our love and passion strengthened through the words written over the many months and miles that separated us.

September 5, 1973, "Jeff, I wish I were there to kiss your warm mouth and feel your strong arms around my willing body. But for now, the miles can only be crossed in our minds, so I touch you and caress you in my thoughts and hope, my love, that you can feel it."

October 2, "Pat, I have always stood by you and will remain by your side for the rest of my life. We should treat one another as the most valuable and important thing in our lives and then work from there. You are my love; that is all I really want in life."

October 8, "Jeff, you have shown me love and that is the most precious gift anyone can give."

On December 8, Jeff wrote before his Christmas visit to Sweden, "We will sleep happily again for the first time in many months for we will be in each others' arms. I know I only truly realize the being of my existence through your touch and the response that my touch brings to you. All I need is to hold you in my arms and things will be alright."

December 11, writing on the day before he was to leave the U.S., "I want to hold you and kiss you and sleep that restful satisfied sleep, which I've only known when I've been next to you. The warm sweet taste of your mouth, the soft, smooth feel of your skin, that strong but tender sensation that only comes when we are locked in an embrace. I need to have that feeling and not just write about it anymore. Ten days, just the number of fingers on your two hands, which I need so much. Soon we can put our pens to rest."

"Take care my love and hurry to me. I await your smile. The courage of your tenderness." When Jeff stepped off the train and held me in his arms, the comfort and ease of our love enveloped us. Passion filled our nights and travel filled our days, as we roamed the countryside by bike and train. The days were short at this time of the year, the sun rising at ten in the morning and setting at two in the afternoon, but we welcomed the long nights and found the rhythm of our love unchanged, our love had only grown stronger.

⚭

In the spring of 1974, I returned home from Sweden a weaver. We stayed in Missouri to finish out Jeff's semester and then drove home to live at his parents' farm for the summer.

On June 22, with Jeff's mom and sister present, we were married by the Justice of the Peace in Edgewater Park, New Jersey. After the simple service, we came home, went up to our bedroom, took off our clothes, and made love in the four-poster bed. An hour later, Jeff was out working in the fields bailing hay.

The next day, with my dad, mom and sister present, we had a small reception for our families at his parent's house. I wore a long silk dress, the color of cream, I had sewn for the occasion. It was a good day.

⚭

The euphoric feeling remained with me long after returning from the doctor's office one steamy day during that same summer. After changing into a pair of shorts, I passed Jeff's mom before heading out through the screen door to work in my vegetable garden on the far side of the farm. "Can you tell Jeff I need to talk to him when he comes in for lunch?" I asked her. "It's important."

The last row of peas was weeded when I looked up and saw Jeff walking my way in the distance. Smiling, wiping the beads of sweat off my upper lip with the back of my hand, I stood up straight to watch him cross the tall green fields of rye straw. He was working eighteen-hour days bailing hay, and his body was lean and strong. He was careful, though, to wear leather gloves so his hands remained smooth when he touched me each night as we lay together.

He scooped me up in his arms when he heard the news. He was going to be a dad.

Chapter 2

Vanessa, Charlotte

"Some things are placed on earth to show others how precious each day is."

Charlotte

At the end of August, we packed up our new van and moved back to Columbia, Missouri for Jeff's last year of undergraduate school. Since we had no room where we lived for my sixty-inch Swedish loom, a wedding present from his mom and dad, we set it up at a friend's house in Columbia, so I could weave rugs and await the birth of our baby.

My body responded rapidly to this new life growing inside me and by three months, my belly was round and swollen, which clothing could not conceal. By the end of five months, people on the street were asking me when I was due, since by then my stomach had expanded to quite an enormous size, picture a very large beach ball blown up to capacity.

Dr. Wallace became my obstetrician since he was the only practicing physician in Columbia Missouri using the relatively new Lamaze method of birthing. The end of November came quickly and I was already seven months pregnant when his partner, Dr. Carter, came into the picture.

When he walked into the room, he took a good look at me sitting awkwardly on the table and moved closer as if he was going to tell me a secret. "You must be mistaken about your dates because you're much too big for seven months." "Sorry, but I'm not wrong about my dates. In fact, at five months, I felt two distinct lumps and told Dr. Wallace, but he just brushed it off and said it was going to be a very large baby. Right now, I can hardly sit down without almost laying flat out because my stomach is so enormous and my rib cage feels as if it's bruised with all this activity going on."

I could tell he thought I was a pushy one, reading way too many books about what it was supposed to be like and needing to vent from not being heard. He listened, though, and after ordering a low-grade x-ray, came back into the room with both his index and middle fingers raised high in the air; "Yes, you are carrying twins."

While I must admit we joked about twins when everyone questioned my size, finding out for sure sent a wave of panic through me for a few moments.

"Go home, put your feet up and take it easy," he told me. "We want you to carry them as long as possible."

Actually, my routine had been quite the opposite of what he had just prescribed; adhering to the instructions of his partner, a two-mile walk everyday, with no limit on activity. I felt good, but had to admit to feeling tired lately, especially on that particular morning.

Going home and breaking the news to Jeff was easy. We were both excited, but also somewhat overwhelmed by the prospect of not one, but two babies in a small two-bedroom trailer. We were living on the GI Bill, supplemented now only by Jeff's summer job.

That night, I suddenly awoke. My nightgown and sheets were soaked. Half awake, I slowly maneuvered my enormous stomach over the side of the bed for another of my many nightly trips to the bathroom. This time though, walking back to the comfort of my waiting nest of pillows, there was a trickle of warm fluid flowing down my leg. "Oh no, now I can't stop peeing."

I woke Jeff, who was lost in the surrounding perimeter of the bed, and when he heard my dilemma he responded with the obvious reasoning I apparently lacked at the moment, "I think your water broke."

We waited eight long hours, my contractions now every five minutes, before deciding to call the obstetrician. Besides being eight weeks early and finding out only the day before I was carrying twins, we were in the midst of a roaring blizzard outside. We felt this was enough ammunition to warrant a phone call.

Even after explaining our dilemma to Dr. Wallace, he seemed annoyed we had not waited the prescribed twelve hours and begrudgingly said he would meet us at the hospital. We arrived at eight in the morning. With my contractions fluctuating between five and fifteen minutes, and with my not yet being dilated, we were told this would be a long wait.

The scene outside my hospital room window slowly unfolded. The all-night blizzard had left a snow-covered hillside splashed with reds and blues from the jackets of the seemingly endless line of sledders trickling up and down the hill. I watched them dash to the bottom as we tried to concentrate on my breathing; no easy task since we had only started Lamaze classes the week before and hadn't had much time to practice.

The exhausting day faded into another sleepless night; the contractions not allowing me any rest. We watched the sunrise through the window, the rays heating up the hillside, as tiny patches of cinnamon-colored earth started peeking through. The sun followed its arc as the day dragged on and soon the long, low shadows of afternoon streaked across the hill, exposing a few remaining patches of leaden gray snow.

The changes outside my window only enhanced my realization of how much time had passed. And here I was, still in the same room, the contractions continuing with no substantial progress. Only now, an overwhelming weakness began settling into my body.

Meanwhile, in the rooms on either side of me, it seemed as if a continuous stream of pregnant women came and went. At first they were a distraction; they soon became a frustration. I lost count of how many, but the routine was always the same, new patient, loud cries, commotion, and then silence.

After forty-four hours of unrelenting contractions, I was spent and expressed to anyone who would listen, which was Jeff and whoever else came in the room, that I needed someone, anyone, to do something.

Dr. Carter arrived to relieve his partner. When he came into the room, he looked alarmed. In one breath, he ordered oxygen, an intravenous drip, oxytocin to induce labor, and told the nurse to "start prepping for a caesarian." Finally, something was happening.

The operating room was bone chillingly cold. I had goose bumps all over my body, while the stinging cold only penetrated deeper. I was awake and aware of all the commotion; only my senses were clouded by the lack of three days sleep. I was too weak to be put under general anesthesia and was told not to move as they inserted the epidural needle into my back.

On December 3, at 1:07 in the morning, Baby A, a girl, was delivered by caesarian section, weighing three pounds, two ounces. There was no sound of a baby crying after they removed her from my body; only a distant voice saying it was a girl, as she was rushed away. At 1:09, another girl, Baby B, was taken from my body, weighing four pounds, seven ounces, again not a sound. I was told the babies were alive, but I couldn't see them because of the drapery over my body. The only sound was the commotion as they were rushed from the room.

Nausea came again in deep, dark waves as Dr. Carter removed my appendix and sewed up the gaping hole in my now trembling body. The cold was slowly winning, overtaking my every thought, when all of a sudden a hot, heavy blanket was draped over my entire body, swallowing me up in a luscious heat. Bliss. My shivering gradually seeped away.

Meanwhile, Jeff was anxiously waiting outside the operating room. The doctor would not allow him to come in with me during the surgery, even when we told him Jeff had spent several years working in army intensive care surgical wards and could handle it. He could only watch helplessly as the girls were rushed past him down the hallway, both in the same isolette; their tiny heads peeking through the flannel covers.

Baby B was immediately rushed by ambulance to the University of Missouri Medical Center's Neonatal Intensive Care Unit in respiratory distress. At birth, she had not taken a breath for four minutes, having swallowed some of my amniotic fluid while still inside me. Baby A remained in the isolette in the hospital's nursery.

Back in my room, in the early hours of the morning, we named Baby A Vanessa and Baby B, Charlotte. We didn't know what would happen, but for now we wanted them each to have a name before Jeff left to call our families with the news. Alone in the room, after we cleaned up my blood soaked body and gown, I tried to get some sleep.

Vanessa stayed in the nursery at Boone County Hospital. When I was able to get up to see her, I thought she looked like a baby monkey; so small and helpless, all head, and although we couldn't hold her yet, I could see that her little body would barely fit into the palm of my hand. As Jeff and I stood looking through the nursery window, we overheard a woman commenting how sad she looked under all the lights, so small and helpless. I tried not to cry.

Meanwhile, Charlotte was fifteen minutes away on a respirator with a tube for fluids and antibiotics inserted where her umbilical cord had been attached only hours before. She was barely holding her own. Jeff was told she had a twenty-five percent chance to live. "She's tiny and connected to lots of tubes, but you can see she's a fighter," he told me when he came back from the Medical Center. I could only hang my hope on his words, since I couldn't yet leave the hospital to see her.

My delivery was the opposite of what we had expected and since nothing else had gone as planned, including three days of monumental headaches from the epidural, I was determined to breastfeed no matter what anyone said.

No one at the hospital encouraged me, since neither of the girls could breastfeed at the time. Charlotte was in another hospital hooked up to an IV, and Vanessa was receiving a high fat supplement so she could put on weight as quickly as possible. I was adamant they would be able to breast feed no matter how long it took, and began pumping my breasts every four hours, around the clock, resolved to be ready for the future.

After all the tubes were removed from my body, I left the hospital early, even before being officially released. I needed to see Charlotte. She was only four days old and fighting for her life.

It was frightening as we came through the doors of the University of Missouri's Neonatal Unit. First we had to find her in a sea of very sick babies. They were moved regularly according to how critical they were. When we finally located her in the small, partially enclosed bed, she looked helpless, lying on her back, a respirator tube protruding from her mouth, her chest rising and falling to the beat of the machine.

Little did we know that this room would become all too familiar to us; the frantic activity, the glaring lights day and night, the constant beeping of monitors. Only one thing was missing, the sound of a baby crying.

After a few days, keeping vigil at the two separate hospitals became oddly routine. We had no physical contact with Vanessa as we watched her through the nursery window, curled up in her isolette. We were not allowed in. On the other side of town, Charlotte was still attached to life support and although we could touch her, she seemed unresponsive. We soon learned there would be nothing routine in this journey.

The following afternoon, after leaving Vanessa, we walked through the doors of the Intensive Care Unit, over to Charlotte's isolette and saw that there was another baby lying there in her place. Frantically, we scanned the sea of babies in search of her. From across the room, Jeff waved his arm. Rushing up to her bed, I didn't understand at first glance, but then realized, no wonder we couldn't find her, the ventilator tube was gone. Charlotte was finally breathing on her own. The tension in my body seeped away. She looked stronger already and although she was still receiving all her nutrients and fluids through the intravenous tube in her belly button, her vital signs were stabilizing.

The next day, while waiting for Jeff to come home from classes so we could go to the hospital, I filled the cooler with over twenty-five bottles of frozen breast milk. Still pumping day and night, I knew the girls couldn't use the milk yet, but the premature babies at the hospital could. Before I was finished pumping, I would wear out two handheld breast pumps.

The loud knock at the door startled me. We had very few visitors so I first looked outside the front window and saw that a police car was parked out front. My first thought was that Charlotte was dead. I did not want to open the door. Reluctantly I faced the nervous police officer, looking everywhere but at me. "Boone County Hospital tried to get in touch with you and couldn't get through so they called us. You need to call them immediately." It wasn't Charlotte, it was Vanessa. I went numb.

Right at that moment, Jeff pulled up and we rushed across the street to call on the pay phone; we were still waiting for our phone to be connected. We were told Vanessa had developed a blockage overnight in her small intestines and at that moment she was being transferred by ambulance to the medical center where her sister was.

Jeff and I were silent on the frantic ride to the hospital, both of us too afraid to speak. After a long meeting with several physicians, we were told there were two options: surgery to remove the blockage or a new procedure the University of Pennsylvania had developed called hyper alimentation. The hope was that this experimental intravenous supplement would provide all the necessary nutrients to sustain Vanessa's life while giving her body time to pass the blockage without major surgery. She now weighed only two pounds and we didn't think she could survive a major surgery, so we agreed.

A few hours later, an incision was made in her neck and a central line was placed into a vein where the nutrients would be absorbed directly into her body. Since this procedure was still in the research phase for babies, it was to be used for only five days.

Meanwhile, as we waited, Charlotte began to drink small amounts of my breast milk from a plastic baby bottle, held to her lips through the portholes of her isolette. She was slowly getting stronger.

Five days passed with no stool in sight for Vanessa, but she was tolerating the treatment, so the doctors decided to continue the therapy.

A few days later, a nurse came over while I was feeding Charlotte her bottle through the portholes. "You can take her out and try nursing her if you like." I laughed. "If I like, are you kidding?" Moments later, Charlotte was in my arms trying to nurse. It didn't take long for her to get the swing of it. Me, I was in my glory, one down, one more to go.

On Christmas Eve, Vanessa passed a small, dark, tar-like substance called the meconium stool, which the nurses placed on top of her isolette with a note saying, "Merry Christmas Mom and Dad." It remains our best Christmas present ever.

℮℮

The New Year started out well. Charlotte came home on January third, exactly one month after her birth, weighing only four pounds, seven ounces, exactly what she had weighed at birth. It was wonderful to wake up to a baby in the house, to be able to feed, bathe and hold her whenever I liked. She was always in my sight. What joy she brought to our lives. It made us realize how much we were missing without Vanessa home too.

Every day we took turns going to the hospital to be with Vanessa or staying home with Charlotte. We watched Vanessa in her isolette flailing her tiny fists at anything she could come in contact with, pulling on her tubes with mittened hands, kicking her feet high in the air as she pushed on the porthole windows, fighting every step of the way. She amazed everyone with her will to live. Little did we know then that she would desperately need this incredible determination to fight for the rest of her life.

Soon, like Charlotte, Vanessa began to take minute amounts of breast milk in a bottle we held through the portholes. The day finally came when I was able to take her out and hold her in my arms for the first time. She was all of three pounds, two ounces less than she had weighed at birth.

Her tiny body was covered from head to toe with little ruby red pinpricks, places the nurses had used for drawing blood. It was painful to see, but even more painful for Vanessa.

The little hat came off as I held her and I could see the blonde stubble where weeks ago they had shaved her head for the central line in her neck. All I wanted to do now was hold her close to my body so she could finally rest, hearing the sound of my heartbeat. It was time for her mom to take care of her.

When the nurse came over a few days later and said I could try to breastfeed Vanessa, she commented as she was leaving the room, "Don't be too disappointed if it doesn't happen. She's so small it may be difficult."

I couldn't wait to scoop her up and finally get to try, but not before first wrapping her snugly in a blanket to keep her warm. She quickly freed her tiny arm and waved it in the air as we sat down in a nearby rocking chair. Cradled in my arms, she turned her head from side to side, over and over again, searching with her mouth; the movement against my breast starting my milk to flow. The next time her lips glanced across my nipple dripping with milk, she found the source and drank from me. There is no other feeling like it in the world.

14

Her tired arm came to rest on my chest, as her body relaxed and softened into mine. What a relief to feel the tension leave her body knowing I could now nourish her.

Now, the problem became breastfeeding two babies who were twenty miles apart. Running back and forth to the hospital was wearing me out. The doctors decided we would be able to bring Vanessa home at four pounds, since we had no problem taking care of Charlotte, who came home at only four pounds seven ounces.

On February third, Vanessa tipped the scales at four pounds, the weight at which a baby can begin to regulate his or her own temperature outside of an isolette. That afternoon, Vanessa journeyed home from the hospital and was reunited again with Charlotte. We were finally a family.

In the coming weeks, we discussed with the hospitals how we could pay the bills incurred over the past two months. We had saved enough to pay for a "healthy birth", but being students, we did not have the income, and in our case, the foresight to have gotten health insurance. We devised a payment plan and on Charlotte and Vanessa's fourteenth birthday, we finally paid off the bill.

Chapter 3

Jeff, Vanessa, Charlotte, Pat

"If you fill your days with regrets of yesterday and worries of tomorrow, then you can't spend your hours living for today."

Charlotte

Months passed. Charlotte and Vanessa thrived on my breast milk and when they turned six months old, on the natural foods I began making for them. Our long morning and afternoon walks in the fresh air strengthened all of us. Wherever we went, people always wanted to pick them up and hold them. Twins were not as common then and we often thought to put a sign on the double stroller with all their statistics so we wouldn't have to answer the same questions over and over. But I must admit, they were cute.

They began filling out and by summer we started calling them "chubby cheeks", probably due to their having been breastfed so much. They were flourishing and full of smiles.

As the summer wore on and the temperature rose, I sometimes noticed they had a little wheeze and on hot days, their sweat tasted salty when I kissed them on their foreheads. On some days, I could actually taste salt floating in the air after I removed their clothes. They also had lots of bulky stools. I mentioned this to their doctor and he said not to worry, they looked great and were growing normally.

I wanted to believe him and tried not to dwell on it, but when I kissed other babies, they didn't taste salty. Uneasiness started growing in the back of my mind, which I tried to ignore, but it remained there nonetheless.

Charlotte and Vanessa had had the sweat test for cystic fibrosis soon after birth, when Vanessa developed the intestinal blockage and the doctor explained that this was one of the symptoms associated with this genetic lung disease. For the original test, Jeff and I had to sit in a hot room close to a radiator trying to make them sweat. Because they were so tiny and their sweat glands were not fully developed, there was no sign of sweat, even after several hours, while Jeff and I were soaking wet. The results of the test are based on the amount of salt in the sweat, hence the name sweat test. That test came back negative, but since the doctor had been concerned, I read everything available on cystic fibrosis and knew that tasting salty and wheezing could be symptoms.

๕๒

In the fall of 1975, we moved to Lexington, Kentucky, where Jeff began graduate school at the University. On our first visit with the new pediatrician, I mentioned the occasional wheeze and salty taste to him. As he was answering my question about whether we needed to do another sweat test, I noticed a book on his desk. The book's title was *Cystic Fibrosis*. I tuned back in as he was saying how healthy and happy the babies looked and how statistically they were growing normally so he didn't think it was necessary to do another test. I agreed with him on their health, but I still wanted it done. Coincidence or not, for my own piece of mind, they needed to be tested.

๕๒

This time, after waiting over an hour for the test results, which normally should take about ten minutes, I knew the news was not going to be good. When the doctor entered the room and closed the door behind him, it wasn't. "The test is positive."

Those few words instantly changed our lives.

I knew by heart the grim statistics, especially the last one, no hope of a cure. At the time, the medical profession was not even sure what caused the disease, although it was thought to be a genetic defect, passed down recessively through both parents, a theory later proven true. Each parent had to be a carrier to create the one-in-four chance occurrence of having a child with the disease. Since the girls were identical twins and had the exact same genetic makeup, they both had cystic fibrosis.

Cystic fibrosis prohibits individual cells from processing salt. The symptoms include a buildup of sticky mucus in the lungs, intestines, pancreas and liver. The cells' inability to transport sodium correctly leads to chronic lung infection and congestion, disruption of the function of the pancreas and the inability of most to digest fats. This all eventually leads to death.

Even now it's hard to relate the feelings Jeff and I had at the time. The girls were ten months old and full of smiles. They were our life. They had never once been sick since leaving the hospital. Everyday we saw how happy and full of life they were. How could it be that one moment we were so full of hope, and the next, we were smothered in a blanket of fear?

I immediately thought they would get sick and die. I did not take to my bed, that just is not me, but I cried a lot. Don't get me wrong; I still performed all the duties of a mother for Charlotte and Vanessa, taking care of all their needs and wants. But I just couldn't feel anything but an overwhelming sadness hanging over me. Just days before, I was living a happy, rewarding life and now I was scared and in a daze.

After a week or two, I realized I couldn't go on like this. Jeff was dealing with so much already, trying to be helpful while working at the thoroughbred stallion station, studying for his degree in veterinary science and trying to cope with the news too.

The following day, I called the hospital and asked if there was someone I could speak to about my situation. They arranged a meeting with a counselor that afternoon. When I told him I was scared to love my own daughters, I couldn't believe I was actually saying those words to him, but it was exactly how I was feeling and I was ashamed and afraid.

It is amazing how quickly your mind and emotions can adjust to how you look at life, especially during a crisis. It took just one visit for me to start feeling my way through the shock and the realization of what we were up against and how I was going to deal with it. The fact that Charlotte and Vanessa had cystic fibrosis could not be changed; how I would deal with it could be changed.

When I arrived at our apartment after my appointment and walked through the door, I was greeted with three big smiles, Jeff's included. At that moment, the girls and Jeff were happy and healthy. That was all I wanted so why shouldn't we again enjoy the time we had together?

I began to realize that if I couldn't change the fact that they had cystic fibrosis, I would try to change the outcome by doing my best to keep them healthy. I would fight this battle using what I knew, nutrition as my weapon.

From then on, I tried to appreciate each day. I relished being a mom, the long walks in the morning and afternoon, bathing and reading to them each night, taking care of all their needs. My days were full and satisfying.

We left Lexington Kentucky in December, two months after their diagnosis. Jeff never completed his master's degree. We decided we did not have the comfort of time anymore. The path of our lives had been chosen and Jeff felt he needed a job that could support and care for us. We wanted to enjoy the days we had together, however many that would be.

Chapter 4

"They told my parents, 'Give them a good life because they probably won't live to be ten years old.' So what has kept us healthy, the love and nourishment from our parents. When they found out we had CF, my dad quit school because he knew he wanted a job that meant he could be home with us. My mom did all the cooking from scratch. All she did was do the cooking and make sure we took all our vitamins. She was up on everything, especially anything holistic and she tried it all out on us."

Vanessa

We moved back home to Philadelphia to be near our families and to have access to one of the best and most innovative cystic fibrosis clinics in the country. We were excited to know the girls would have the best care available, but it was a rocky start.

At our first visit, we discussed how the girls were flourishing with their walks, their healthy diet and supplemental enzymes and vitamins to help them digest their food properly. Everything was going fine until we were told that all cystic fibrosis patients, healthy or not, were started on antibiotics to keep infections at bay. We immediately said no, we did not want to use antibiotics until the girls needed them, knowing the implications of constant use.

We were adamant, asking why we should begin antibiotics, risking a resistance against future infections, when they were obviously healthy and thriving. All the doctors had to do was look at the girls and see that something was working, and I wasn't changing their care for a policy. After much discussion, we said that if necessary, we would go to another center and then finally they deemed it okay that the girls be treated at the clinic without their starting on antibiotics.

Years later, this treatment policy was dropped because of the resistance that developed quickly to each antibiotic and the constant need for stronger and stronger ones. When we finally resolved that issue, the clinic said I needed to discontinue the girls' vitamins because they were not part of the hospital's treatment program. Again I said no, that although I knew they hadn't been proven to work in any laboratory yet, they obviously helped the girls, and again why would I change what was working? They told me that they did not agree, but there was nothing they could do to stop us from continuing the supplements in their diet. Ten years later vitamins became part of the cystic fibrosis nutritional program.

St. Christopher's turned out to be an exceptional center, but this experience made me realize that as the girls' mom, I would have to stand up for them no matter what. I knew their bodies better than anyone, as they would themselves know them later in life. I also knew that staying healthy would require a team effort with the physicians, not compliance to something I did not agree with. Working together and listening to one another is critical when fighting for your life, or a loved one's life. I quickly learned how important it was to be informed and not to remain silent.

~ ❧ ~

We quickly settled into the second floor of a house in Bordentown, New Jersey, when the rambunctious girls were two years old. They immediately took over the sunny porch, which was bordered in windows, and filled it with their toys, joys and laughter.

Jeff decided to try his hand in the thoroughbred horse racing business. He grew up around horses with his father in the business for thirty years and had been studying equine medicine in graduate school. It was something he knew well and liked, so he started working with his brother Bob, who trained horses for several owners at Philadelphia Park racetrack.

In 1978, Mr. Keenan, one of the horse owners, told Jeff he had purchased a farm in Chester County and was looking for a farm manager. Since we were looking for a real home for Charlotte and Vanessa, who were now four-years-old, Jeff told him he was interested.

⊘⊘

On a warm, sunny, crystal clear day in August, we all piled into Mr. Keenan's car to visit the newly purchased farm in Chester County. Jeff and Mr. Keenan sat up in the front seat, the girls and I in the back. Forty-five minutes later, we turned off of Route 202 and began to make our way along a narrow winding road into the countryside. The lush ceiling of trees and vines was so thick the sunlight barely peeked through, creating abstract patterns on the road as we wound our way around a sharp bend and slowly ascended a rise in the road.

Suddenly, the view expanded and the valley with its gently rolling hills was spread before us. There were a few farmhouses, fenced-in fields and barns, and horses dotting the pea-green pastures. The car slowly climbed a long, steep hill, past two white churches and an ancient cemetery. At the top of the hill stood the entrance to the farm, graced by two stone pillars and several large fields of tall rye grass as far as the eye could see. The girls and I looked at one another. We could scarcely contain our excitement.

The long driveway overlooking the valley wound past fields and fences until we came to a fork in the road where there was an enormous old oak tree, its trunk splintered and partially burned from a lightning strike. The "witch's tree" the girls would call it, until several years later when a summer storm split it in two, creating enough firewood for many cold nights.

We continued on past the tree, down a steep hill, rounding a corner near the stone garage, the stable and a paddock tucked in the woods. We followed the low stone wall until we came to the eighteenth-century, ivy-covered stone farmhouse. Standing guard near the front entrance was an old sinuous Japanese split leaf maple tree, laden with feathery lime green leaves, its twisted branches hidden under the lush foliage.

When the car stopped, Charlotte and Vanessa jumped out, ran to the front door and waited patiently for us to come up the massive stone walk. After opening the front door, we stepped into a broad hall dominated by a staircase. The girls scrambled past us and raced up the steps as fast as their little legs would carry them, choosing opposite directions at the landing. We stayed to explore the downstairs.

The living room was five times as long as it was wide and at the far end was a huge walk-in fireplace. Along plaster covered stone walls two feet in depth, were recessed windows overlooking the woods. In the adjoining library, wooden bookcases lined the walls and a small fireplace completed the scene. In all, the house had five fireplaces, something we would cherish in the many winters to come. The farmhouse kitchen had a big picture window overlooking the original springhouse nestled down by the spring and creek. Many wonderful dinners with friends and family would originate from this kitchen.

When we made our way up to the second floor, we found three large bedrooms and one bath. By the time we arrived upstairs, the girls had already picked out the room they wanted to share; the smallest of the three but with a large closet they already decided could be transformed into a secret hideaway. The attic on the third floor contained three big unfinished rooms.

As Jeff and I headed back down the steps from the third floor, all we had to do was look at one another to know that this was what we had been searching for; a special place to build our life together with the girls. This was to become our sanctuary.

Chapter 5

Charlotte, Vanessa

"Imagine being a child living in your own magical kingdom, with
mystical streams, enchanted forests, and your own little castle, shared
with your best friend. By day you search in streams for fat frogs and
slippery salamanders, lie in the cool clover under ripening pear trees,
hoping that one may drop so you can have a scrumptious treat. By
night, you would catch lightning bugs to put in a jar for a lantern,
illuminating each other's face in the dark. And finally when it was time
to dream, songs of the crickets would lull you to sleep. These fairy-time
images make up the memories of my childhood. It was a time when all
my dreams seemed in reach."

Charlotte

O n September 15, 1978, Charlotte, Vanessa and I moved to
the one hundred and forty-acre farm. They were three and
a half years old. Since the girls could not be exposed to paint
fumes and dust, Jeff, my brother and my parents had already been at the
farm for two weeks without the girls and me, working fifteen-hour days
getting the house ready for us to move into.

From the moment of our arrival, we were enchanted. It was all we had ever hoped for, nestled in the rolling hills of Chester Springs, Pennsylvania. "God's country," my dad came to call it.

The first year we hardly left the property, working hard and taking time to explore the new-found wonders of the ever-changing farm and woods. Our daily walks were magical. Springs bubbled up through the dark earth, joining together to form icy cold streams. Smells were intoxicating, damp and musty one minute, warm and sweet the next. Almost everyday, we pulled on our boots and set out on adventures exploring the woods and fields.

Near the house, attached to the open stable, was a large room that became the girls' very own magical playhouse and refuge, always filled with lots of giggles as well as serious play. Fanciful stories were concocted here, kings and queens held court, plays and puppet shows were perfected and performed, rules were made and broken, oaths were sworn in secrecy as friends became blood sisters. A stuffed animal hospital was established in this room, helping the girls understand their illness through play.

By now my parents were coming down from their home in New Jersey most weekends. They loved the peace that enveloped this place, especially the abandoned springhouse located a few hundred yards from the house. At dinner during one of these visits, my dad began talking about his approaching retirement. "We would like to fix up the springhouse so that when I retire we can move here to be near to you and the girls. We also could help Jeff out around the farm." Knowing how hard they both had worked throughout their lives, we knew they would find some happiness here and the girls were thrilled with the prospect of having their nanny and pop pop so close by. We agreed to talk to Mr. Keenan about it.

That night after dinner, we all walked down to look around the springhouse and consider the possibilities. My dad loved old things. He could see beyond the low-hanging branches of the weeping willow tree that lay across what little roof remained, beyond the rotting wooden floor covered with a sea of black walnuts the industrious squirrels had gathered for winter storage, and beyond the gaping dark holes where the windows and doors used to be. Through all the decay, he could see the strong, sound foundation beneath, much like his own.

Years before, the springhouse had been used as the kitchen for the main house and the large brick oven was still intact. Before refrigeration, the room under the first floor kept perishables cool in the hot summer months with the icy spring flowing around its edges. The water encircled the room in a trough before passing through a small hole in the far stone wall, emptying into a spring-fed stream, filled with moss-covered stones and tasty watercress growing on its banks.

Besides reading, music and history, fixing up old houses was what gave my dad joy in life. Every house we had ever lived in had his signature; each was shaped by my father's strong hands, the hands I see every time I look at my own. He could mend a broken doll or lay a hardwood floor, whatever was needed. He knew this would be a big job, but he loved the idea of turning this shell of a building into something useful again.

We spoke to Mr. Keenan and it was agreed that my dad and mom would cover all of the costs of materials and provide the labor to fix up the house. In return, they could live there for as long as they lived or the farm was sold, which he said would never happen because he considered it "the family farm."

Looking back, I now know we were all very naïve to put our trust in a verbal agreement with so much at stake, but we trusted Mr. Keenan and believed he was telling us the truth when he said over and over again that we were part of his family.

Nevertheless, at the beginning of the summer of 1979, my parents started to make their dream a reality. They came down every weekend, the car loaded with groceries and tools so they could work on the house, help out around the farm and spend time with the girls. My dad especially loved the peace and solitude he found here. My mom enjoyed being together with all of us.

The following year, my dad retired and for the next year, while my parents lived on the third floor of our house, he and my mom worked every day on the springhouse. Inside walls were built, huge stones were painstakingly removed from both ends of the top of the house so air could circulate under the roof, and he laid new hardwood floors. It took well over a year, but when it was finished it was magnificent, from the spacious kitchen with the original stone walk-in fireplace and bake oven, all the way back to the snug bedroom, tucked behind a wall of handmade bookcases. Everything was custom made by my dad, even the screens for the small windows, including the latches to open them. My mom worked by his side most days and as the house neared completion, she took care of all the finishing touches to make it home. The empty shell had been transformed into a graceful, cozy cottage.

∂ß

In the meantime, the farm was growing by leaps and bounds. Horses were being bred, bought and sold in Kentucky, Maryland, and Virginia. Jeff had over fifty horses on the farm to care for, mostly mares and foals, but also some boarders from the racetrack. He was also building barns, clearing land, and fencing paddocks. This was a seven-day a week, twenty-four hour a day job and we loved it.

Foaling season began in January and ended most years in May, meaning Jeff slept in the barn many nights from January to May, awaiting the birth of a foal. A running joke was that the mares knew someone was watching because many of the foals were born when Jeff would come down for dinner, after sleeping for weeks in the barn awaiting the birth. We also spent some sleepless nights taking care of a sick mare or foal, or spent some days picking dandelion greens because that was the only food the sick mare would eat.

When Jeff wasn't caring for the horses, he was maintaining and improving the grounds. The days were long and arduous, but he loved the horses, loved working with his hands and believed he was building our future.

All in all it was a wonderful life, allowing us to give the girls a magical childhood; in fact, it gave us all a magical look at life.

Chapter 6

Vanessa, Charlotte

"It was the most amazing childhood growing up on a horse farm. We picked raspberries with my mom, Pop Pop and Nanny. Just all the love and having them there and not having any stress. They were always playing with us. My dad and mom were on the farm all day long, so we could always see them. It was a great childhood; it was truly amazing. It was a great atmosphere. My mom would cook great meals every night, we had my Nan and Pop Pop living on the farm, we would all take walks every night. Everything was for the day."

Charlotte

Our life together was good and although Jeff's salary was not large, everyday life on the farm made up for that. Knowing what lay ahead was a constant reminder that we should be living day to day, trying to make each one count. A simple cold was never taken lightly. The girls' daily medical routine, even when they were healthy, included morning and night medicated nebulizer treatments and postural drainage or clapping on their chests in many different positions to loosen the mucus in their lungs. All meals included the constant supply of vitamins and enzymes to help them digest their food.

Their illness was never far from our thoughts; especially around the holidays when each year we wondered if this might be the last one we all would share together. But for the most part, we were very grateful for the life we had made together.

At the end of most summer days, we took long walks after dinner. The girls always ran up ahead, laughing and climbing the fence to pet the horses, who nuzzled up to have their ears scratched or to grab a bite of carrot or apple held out in the palm of the girls' hands, the smell of sweet oats and saliva left behind as a thank you.

Several days a week the girls, my mom and I would go to the local dairy with our pails for the raw milk we used in making yogurt, cheese and for just plain drinking. The large stainless steel tanks, filled with swirling milk, were in a small barn off the larger one used to house the cows when they came in from the fields to be milked. We placed the pails, one at a time, beneath the spigot of the tank and turned it on until we could see and smell the sweet bubbles of warm milk rising to the top. When the pails were full, we turned off the spigot, put the lid on the pails and as we left, placed one dollar and twenty-five cents for each gallon in the small metal box by the barn door. By the time we were home, the thick, luscious yellow cream had already settled on top.

When I wasn't preparing meals, making pasta, cheese or bread, or working in my garden, my mom and I worked as a team, sewing and knitting most of the girls' clothes. Sometimes, I would spin and dye the wool for a special hat or sweater and my mom would start knitting away. The quick, methodical click of her needles would be heard until she completed her task, which never took long. She could knit like a machine.

When spring arrived, Charlotte and Vanessa loved to help me gather plants, such as May apple and Jack in the Pulpit, in the woods surrounding the house. We used them in the dye pot set up for the summer in the back yard. The plants would simmer in a large pot of water long enough for the color to be extracted, then we removed the plant material and added the mordant used to cause the dye to adhere to the wool. Then, it was time for the magic to begin.

As we immersed the long skeins of white wool in the pot, we watched them slowly turn a deep hue of yellow or green, depending on the plant and mordant used. After the yarn absorbed all the color, we would rinse it several times until it ran clear and then hang it out to dry on the clothesline tied between two trees; the same clothesline we used to dry our towels and sheets in the summer. I love the smell of laundry dried in the sun and fresh air, there is nothing like it.

When the skeins of yarn were dry, we would roll them into balls, one person holding the skein between their outstretched arms and the other winding the ball. It was then ready to be knit or woven into something special.

As summer rolled around our huge garden had already been providing us with lots of asparagus and spring vegetables, while the summer plants were readying their bounty for picking. We all spent time tending the garden for our everyday meals and although the girls were never enamored with the thought of pulling weeds, they loved picking the green beans and zucchini and tomatoes and corn as they ripened over the summer. Most years we were lucky enough to have plenty left over to freeze and enjoy during the winter months.

Sugar snap peas were their favorite, ready to be picked in late spring. Charlotte and Vanessa would start at one end of the white string fence we had constructed, their little hands scouring the vines for the plump, tender pea pockets filled with sweet morsels. They usually popped as many pods into their mouths as they gathered in their baskets, but there was always plenty left over for dinner; the girls' portion left uncooked. They never did acquire a taste for cooked snap peas or most vegetables for that matter.

I loved this life.

Chapter 7

Vanessa, Charlotte

"I was young and on the routine walk home from the bus stop, the air was thick and clung to my skin. Surrounded by the sweet odor of damp cut grass and freshly blooming daffodils, I stopped to pick some daffodils as the pungent smell swirled about my head, making the remainder of my walk a floating cloud of spring fever."

Vanessa

I can still close my eyes and smell the seasons drifting slowly by at the farm. Spring meant hundreds of red tulips, lemon-scented daffodils and grass that smelled of onions. As the early spring flowers began to fade, the pale pink viburnum bush burst into bloom, releasing its sweet, grandmotherly scent through my open kitchen window. On our long evening walks, the perfume of magnolia, dogwood and cherry blossoms mingled with each passing breeze, filling the air with their heavenly scent.

One year the girls surprised me with a lavender-colored lilac bush on Mother's Day, my favorite spring flower. I love the smell; fragrances can take me to many places in my life and I love that. Jeff says I am half bloodhound and he may be right.

We planted it near the bend in the driveway, right by their fort, a place I could see from my bedroom window. Although the garden center said it would take several years to flower, the following spring it supplied us with clusters of fragrant flowers that we placed next to our beds so we could enjoy the scent as we drifted off to sleep at night. Within a few years, it became a hedge of fragrant flowers we looked forward to each spring.

Summer was our favorite time of year; a time when fireflies filled the air on sultry summer nights and crickets were never silent. Charlotte and Vanessa had nothing to do all day but play, restrained by nothing and inspired by unbridled daydreaming.

Usually their day started early as they filled their tummies with a big breakfast; buttermilk pancakes with blueberries and maple syrup was one of their favorites. After breakfast they were outside playing most of the day, stopping only for lunch, pedaling their bicycles around the farm, riding their pony, Hoover, in the back paddock, spending the day in their fort with Hershey their chocolate lab and her pup Godiva, performing operations on their stuffed animals, building dams in the stream, walking in the woods to the witches' den, or practicing a play for days on end and then performing it for whoever was there to watch. The possibilities were endless.

This routine was interrupted only by our time in Ocean City, New Jersey, when we would visit Jeff's family for a few weeks, taking in the sun and beach. The girls always loved this respite and all the friends they made at the beach, some friendships lasting into adulthood.

❧

When Charlotte and Vanessa turned nine years old, Jeff built them a tree house. It was in the shape of a triangle, built to fit between three black walnut trees, the floor large enough for two sleeping bags. He built a ten-foot high ladder so we could all climb into the house through a small opening in the floor. We hung a turquoise tarp across a taut rope to shape a peaked roof with walls ending about three feet above the floor, allowing cool breezes to flow over the floor, carrying the sound of crickets, cicadas and sometimes at night, the bark of a fox. It became a special place for us all that summer and for many summers to come.

Sometimes on moonlit nights, after the girls were asleep in their own beds, Jeff and I retreated to the tree house with a bottle of champagne and our sleeping bags in tow. The smell of freshly cut grass and a sky filled with stars was all we needed on those warm summer nights.

✣✣

Fall inevitably arrived each year and with it the routine of school and whatever sport the girls decided to participate in that year. Over the years, they played softball, lacrosse and soccer, which Jeff coached for several years.

We always had a nature project going and every fall Charlotte, Vanessa and I would go into the woods and see how many colors and varieties of leaves we could find. We enjoyed the musky scent of fall at our fingertips as we emptied the contents of the baskets onto the kitchen table, sorting the leaves according to the type of tree and choosing the most colorful ones to keep. We then placed each leaf between pieces of waxed paper and quickly ironed the paper until it was flat and tightly sealed. When it cooled, we carefully cut around each leaf, making sure not to break the seal, glued it to a piece of construction paper, labeled it, and assembled the pages into a book, punched holes down the side, and threaded a cord through the holes to bind it. We never grew tired of this and we made a new book each year.

As winter approached on the farm, a welcome stillness settled over our lives. The fireplaces burned day and night, and outside, musty wet smells intermingled with the scent of lichen-covered burning wood, which added a spicy sweet smell to the mix.

The bedtime routine changed ever so slightly. We all sat down to dinner earlier now and baths soon followed. Then the girls climbed into their pajamas, but instead of getting tucked into bed for their stories, we all cuddled up on the sofa in front of a roaring fire, tended by Jeff, who believes the bigger the fire, the better it is. There, nestled close together with the warmth of the fire drifting over us, sleep came easily after several stories.

Winter brought Christmas, the girls' favorite holiday. The house smelled of pine and spices from baking cookies, breads and cakes, some to keep and some to give away. We strung long strands of garland with cranberries and popcorn to wrap around the newly cut Christmas tree and gathered fresh greens from the woods to weave into wreaths to hang on the doors and over fireplaces.

On Christmas Eve, the girls huddled close to Jeff as he helped write the note they composed to Santa, placed beside the cookies and milk right next to the fireplace so Santa wouldn't miss it. The last story read before bed was The Night Before Christmas, as they tried to close their eyes while we kissed them goodnight and chimed our nightly refrain. "Good night, sleep tight, don't let the bed bugs bite. See you in the morning light. See you later alligator, after awhile, crocodile."

They awoke early on Christmas Day and would quietly wait on the stairs until we sleepily appeared. The first thing they did as they ran down the stairs was to see if the cookies and milk were gone and read the note left by Santa on the empty plate. Even when they didn't believe in Santa Claus anymore, they still put out the cookies and milk next to the fireplace with a note, always expecting one in return.

Only after they had read the note would they head for the fireplace to look for goodies in the needlepoint stockings I had made for them when they were babies. They had to dig down deep to get the last of the surprises before moving on to their presents under the tree. Then it was a big breakfast and in the afternoon, we would head to Grandma's house for Christmas dinner with the family.

✂☙

Over the years, the passage of time was marked by the one-hundred-and fifty-year-old split leaf Japanese maple tree as it changed with the seasons.

Spring brought tender green leaves and delicate seedpods onto its branches, creating a cool, lush canopy for summertime climbing. As summer faded into fall and the nights grew colder, the leaves turned a brilliant red, yellow and orange, colors so intense the tree seemed on fire.

As winter approached and the days were shorter, the leaves withered and fell to the ground, exposing the dark, unyielding trunk and the low, snakelike branches, thick as a slender woman's thigh, meandering upwards into tips as delicate as her hairpins, each branch taking on a life of its own, twisting and turning, creating a living sculpture at rest.

Soon, the long shadows of winter retreated and when every other living thing was still in hiding, tiny white snowdrops and glory-of-the-snow wildflowers appeared under the tree's bare branches, bringing renewed hope that spring was not far off. Throughout the year, this tree became the embodiment of change and renewal for me, a strong, slender thread of hope and continuity in our very fragile lives.

Chapter 8

Vanessa, Charlotte

"Summers on the farm were a mixture of smells and tastes that permeate the subconscious. This was raspberry season and we had our battle gear ready. Pop Pop had fashioned together the armor that would protect us from our three greatest enemies when gathering berries, bugs, prickles, and poison ivy. Vanessa and I pulled on our khaki pants, long sleeve shirts and gloves and raced downstairs. "Girls, you can't go berry picking without one of these," Pop Pop would call out from his basement workshop. It was here that he kept his myriad of tools and jars of every kind of nut and bolt, where it smelled of duct tape and grease. It was the oldest room in the house, with a floor consisting of dirt and gravel. His tools hung from the upstairs floor rafters and from pegs he had made at his large workbench. I spent many hours outside this room waiting for Pop Pop to work his magic on my many broken dolls and toys. He always succeeded with a smile. The operation would be a success; his enthusiasm let me look past the glue to the repaired patient. This time Pop Pop emerged with two hats, one for Vanessa and one for me. The hats were old and worn with mosquito netting hanging from the brim, fastened to the front with yellow string, which made your fingers yellow when you touched it and left a thin yellow line under your chin, but they were perfect to ward off pesky insects. We all grabbed our buckets,

*I*t was the end of June, the time when plump ripe raspberries, warm from the sun, were reaching their peak and serious berry picking time was fast approaching. If you watched closely, you'd see that everyone has their own style of picking.

The girls and I always loved the taste of the first few berries in our mouths, warm and luscious, each small module bursting open with sweetness on our tongues; there was nothing else quite like it. Our method was to eat a few and pick a few until we grew tired of the mosquitoes, flies and brambles. Most of the time this was within the first hour or two, sometimes sooner.

My father, on the other hand, would rarely eat any berries; he would be on a mission to pick as many as possible, losing none to his mouth. Filling his bucket to the top was the goal, sometimes lasting all day, but he would come back satisfied when the job was accomplished. On most days the bucket came back full, ready to be eaten for dessert that night with either Breyers vanilla ice cream or whipped cream or both.

The problem was that my dad accomplished his mission with a generous use of bug spray. He would rub it on his face to keep the flies away, although they still always managed to get under the netting of his hat and irritate him while he was trying to pick. He had no tolerance for these pests; so, much to my consternation, he applied the liquid bug spray in copious amounts.

One day he went out on an all day excursion, gone from midmorning until late afternoon. He came back with two buckets filled to the brim, looking extremely satisfied as he set the stainless steel buckets down on the porch, ready for eating. As I came closer, the strong smell of bug spray overpowered me. I peered into the buckets and saw an oily film flicker in the low afternoon sun. As my dad turned to leave, I asked him about it. "Oh, just a little bug spray spilled in. You can wash them off and they should be fine."

Peering into the buckets, I knew they were beyond washing. They had already lost their berry identity by collapsing from a tight red cluster bound together, into tiny round separate beads; the buckets were filled not with whole berries, but with only the small parts. I took the buckets inside and futilely tried washing handfuls of the beads. But to no avail, his long day of berry picking had disappeared down the drain; his day of work was not salvageable. Needless to say, there were no berries for the ice cream that night, but thankfully my dad never again used bug spray around the berries again.

Chapter 9

Vanessa, Megan, Charlotte

"Lungs are a perfect nesting ground for bacteria. It's moist with lots of mucus. They lodge in there and say, 'Ahhh, this is a nice place to live, vacation time.' And then they just take over."

Vanessa

Charlotte and Vanessa were seven years old when they were hospitalized for the first time. They were coughing more than usual and their mucus looked thicker and darker. The x-ray confirmed pneumonia in both the girls' lungs. As Dr. Schidlow, who is known for singing opera in the hospital elevator, was showing us the film he said, "Look at this, it's amazing, they both have pneumonia in the exact same place, the lower right hand lobe."

They were admitted into the hospital and we arranged to have them in their own room so I could help take care of them.

The first few nights I stayed with them, but after a few days of getting them adjusted to their new surroundings and routine, I started going home at night. I would arrive at the hospital about 6:30 am, just as they woke up and leave after they had their last story and were tucked into bed. Since they were in their own room, I kept the door closed and tried to keep up some semblance of a normal life during the day. Puzzles, games and lots of stories were how we passed the time in between their being poked and prodded with intravenous antibiotics flowing into their bodies and respiratory/percussion treatments four times a day.

After they fell asleep at night, I would drive the hour or so home and would cook for them, since the hospital food was not very appealing and they needed to gain weight to fight the infection. This way they ate well and I felt I could lend a hand in their recovery.

The drive home became a respite for me. Exiting the expressway, I'd roll down the car window and take long deep breaths, filling my lungs with the cold night air, enjoying the wind across my face, washing away the tired hospital air that permeated through me, grateful to escape into this quiet solitude, fortunate to feel this simple pleasure in life.

Chapter 10

Pat, Vanessa, Charlotte

"We had these huge vacations. It is so funny because I always thought we were rich, because of the way we lived and I later found out we were, but not with money. And even when they didn't have much money my mom and dad would scrimp together money to take us places, like friends' houses on the Outer Banks of North Carolina and in the Adirondacks."

Charlotte

At the end of two weeks in the hospital, we took the girls' home. They were tired but much improved. We decided some warm sun and fun was needed, so we packed up and on the recommendation of a travel agent, went to Marco Island, Florida, known for its beaches. The sun there was not as cooperative as we would have liked, but the condominium was on the beach, so long walks, big breakfasts and lots of good food put some much-needed weight on the girls, five pounds each to be exact.

On a few of the days we drove two hours east to Miami where the sun was shining. We visited the Metro Zoo, Parrot Jungle and other attractions. The sun always started to peek through when we were about halfway across the state, but we couldn't stop to catch the rays; this was the Everglades for as far as the eye could see, inhabited by alligators and swampland, so we just kept on driving.

All in all it was a good trip. The girls' health returned and everything went back to normal. It was then we decided that a yearly trip to the sun was the ticket to good health, so that is what we saved for.

Of all the big vacations we took as a family, even counting the ones to Disney World, Casa de Campo in the Dominican Republic remained Charlotte and Vanessa's favorite family vacation.

We went there the first time when the girls were ten. We arrived after a long flight from New York, touching down in Santa Domingo. The passengers were literally clapping and shouting for joy; needless to say it was an exciting flight. When making the reservation, I requested a room with a view of the ocean and since it was right before the high season, the rate was one-third the normal cost. It was dark by the time we checked in and piled the girls into the golf cart, dolls and luggage in tow, to find our room.

When we arrived at the address, we saw that it was a house not a room as we expected. The interior was huge, wrapped entirely in honey-colored mahogany. The three large bedrooms, tile floors and several terraced balconies radiated out from the open-air living room. We immediately thought there was a mix-up in the reservation, but it was late and we were exhausted so we decided to deal with the matter in the morning.

"Mommy, there is a man in the house," Charlotte half whispered, half screamed, as the girls came running into our room in the morning. "He's in the kitchen." We jolted awake and Jeff went to investigate. When he returned he told us it was Domingo, the gardener, who spoke little English.

After several minutes on the phone, we learned that this property was reserved for us because we had requested an ocean view and only houses had ocean views. Domingo, the gardener, and Amada, the cook, were the staff of the family who owned the house and they were available to us. In the coming days, Domingo introduced Charlotte and Vanessa to the island's magic, all in our own back yard.

Domingo had a young daughter so he was happy when the girls followed him around the yard, helping to pick grapefruit and oranges from the abundant trees. Amada then cut up the fruit for us all to enjoy. The meals she made were delicious and always more than enough was left over for them to take home to their families.

One day, we ventured out for a day of snorkeling on a one hundred and twenty-foot wooden sailing ship. The water was sparkling as we headed out to sea, our destination a coral reef a few hours away. We ate a leisurely lunch on deck as we neared the reef where we could snorkel. The girls had lots of fun sharing their boxes of raisins with the crew who had never eaten raisins out of little boxes before. We slowed to a stop and dropped anchor not far from a small island, deemed off limits; it seemed the enticing sandy white beach was swarming with mosquitoes. Our destination was not the island, but the colorful coral reef below the boat.

Everyone was relaxing in the sun after lunch, waiting to find the energy to don our gear and start snorkeling, when all of a sudden I saw the girls in their fearless partnership, jump over the side of the boat, snorkels held high in their hands; it was a long way down and they were not strong swimmers. Needless to say, they were in way over their heads, so Jeff and I quickly jumped in after them.

After making sure they had made the flight down to the water's surface okay, we got them each a raft so they could stay afloat when they grew tired. They were in their glory. We saw stingrays, octopus, fish of all colors and shapes, and a rich variety of coral.

On and off the boat, Jeff and I were shown once again how the girls found strength in their twin-hood. They did not fear much in life, perhaps because they had each other and found comfort in that intimacy and companionship. They really did take care of one another in a very profound way.

As young children, their communication was their own, innate and primal, which seemed to feed their souls. It made them fear little and bolstered their sense of strength and influence; rarely did they remain in the background in play or in life, but commanded everyone's attention by the sheer vivaciousness and passion they brought to everything they did. They exuded life.

Chapter 11

Pop Pop, Charlotte, Vanessa, Nan

"It didn't matter if I brought him a bouquet of weeds, which I frequently did, he would treat them like roses. Every picture I drew was a work of art, every story I told was of utmost importance; everything I found was pure gold. But most importantly, I remember the way he gazed at me, proud and with totally unconditional love. His hands were those of a man who had worked hard all his life, yet these wrinkled, tired old hands were baby soft to the touch because it was the touch of love. This strong sacrificing man was my grandfather.

The memories form vivid images: picking pockets full of ripe red raspberries on a hot sweaty summer day, riding bikes along worn paths on the farm, walking by his side to the little church at the farm's edge, voyaging to the small graveyard overlooking the valley and walking the rows reading the stones of peoples lives, our weekly trips to Camp Hill, the organic farm, where we sipped soup in the small café. He played the role of a perfect audience to our plays, clapping and laughing wildly throughout. He made it his job and desire to look out for us and to make sure that there were always smiles on our faces and that our childhood was being lived to its fullest."

Charlotte

*I*n the fall of 1982, we found out my dad had prostate cancer, which
had already spread to his bones. He was given six months to live. He
fought hard, trying alternative treatments along with conventional
medicine and responded to each for a while, living another four years.
During the last few months of his life, not able to do much except
silently endure the pain, he lost his hearing due to a blood clot in the
back of his brain. Now music, one of the only pleasures left to him, was
suddenly gone too.

The night before the surgery for the blood clot, I watched my
father's eyes fill with tears as he read the letter I gave him. I needed him
to know how important he was in my life and since he couldn't hear me,
I wrote it down. I wish then I had known more about dying so I could
have helped him on his journey.

❧

My dad had worked hard his whole life. When he was nine, he found
his dad and brother dead on the floor of their house from a gas leak,
and when he turned twelve, his mother died of stomach cancer. He
quit school so he could help take care of his four sisters. He joined the
army during World War II and was stationed in New Guinea. He met
my mom when he was on leave in Australia and she became a war bride
soon after. My brother John and my sister Jan were born over the next
two years in Australia. Two years after the war, they all came to the
United States on a war bride ship.

While we were growing up, my dad sometimes worked three jobs
to support us, always working, if not at his job, then at home fixing up
the house. Looking back, I never felt we lacked for much. He always
worked hard to give us what he could and sometimes that meant the last
dime in his pocket for an ice cream from the truck that came around the
neighborhood. He was not a physically or emotionally demonstrative
person, but deep down he had a very warm, soft center.

❧

My dad never regained consciousness after the surgery. When the operation was over the surgeon informed me that my dad would live only
another twenty-four hours. They didn't know how strong his heart was,

it just wouldn't give up, perhaps it was the years of yoga he and my mom did every day.

My mom and I spent our time at the hospital while John, my brother from Australia, my brother Jeff who was in the Navy somewhere in the Middle East, and my sister Jan from California made arrangements to come.

A week passed before we all gathered in his hospital room to say good-bye and even though they said he was not conscious of us, I felt him squeeze my hand ever so slightly as we spoke. A few hours later, with all of us around him, he breathed his last breath.

My dad was buried on June 12, 1986, in the cemetery next to the farm. Each spring, against the bleached white tombstones, thousands of mountain pinks burst into bloom, taking one's breath away. This was the special place we had walked together in the evening with the girls, reading epitaphs aloud from years long ago. I was glad he would be close to the land he loved and we could easily visit.

୪୧

A journey of my own began soon after. The girls doctor thought I should start branching out a little from home so in the fall, I enrolled in an art class at Rosemont College, near Philadelphia. By the end of the semester, I decided to finish my degree.

I had been teaching weaving and selling my handwoven clothing twice a year at a gallery, but most of this work was done in isolation. Going back to school was exactly what I was looking for and after the next semester I was awarded a yearly scholarship to Rosemont as a continuing education student. College brought a rich satisfying element back into my life and I knew I could become a perpetual student; learning is so much fun.

Chapter 12

Charlotte, Vanessa

"Charlotte, where is your homework? The teacher scowls at me. I look her right in the eye and say, "I'm Vanessa," Yet I really don't think she believes me. Although we hardly see a resemblance, most people confuse me with my identical twin sister.

"When picking an ideal word most frequently used to describe me, "unique" comes to mind. Yet to me this seems exceptionally ironic considering I'm an identical twin. Many people ask what it's like being a twin. Well it's not just having a complete replica of one's self, it's always knowing you'll have a best friend, a friend and companion who knows you both inside and out. In fact, my sister steered me into my love of acting."

Vanessa

From the time Charlotte and Vanessa were able to walk and talk, they loved to act. Growing up on the farm gave them lots of creative space where their imaginations could run wild. On weekends and during the summers, the house hummed with the sound of them practicing lines from the plays they had written. They built imaginative sets before presenting the play for Nan, Pop Pop, Jeff and me. If friends happened to be over, the girls were in their glory; they now had an even larger audience to play to.

The routine was generally the same if the play was performed indoors. There was a make shift curtain, hung on a rope or wooden dowel set up across from the couch in the living room. Usually lots of commotion could be heard from behind the curtain as we sat down on the sofa ready for the play or puppet show to begin.

When it did, there would be two introductions. As twins, they always needed equal time. Charlotte, then Vanessa, or vice versa, would each take a turn parting the curtain and describing what was about to transpire.

There were times when the play would go on much longer than anticipated, but if we tried to move from the spot, there was no hesitation on the girls' part to stop what they were doing and admonish the audience. This was serious business.

When we finally saved up enough money to purchase a video camera so they could record their plays and skits, the sound of the girls yelling "quiet on the set" would reverberate throughout the house.

They worked so hard to capture the story, whatever it was. In a scene from a documentary they made for school about the life of Andrew Jackson, a long take on Charlotte's sneer was priceless, as Vanessa, the slave owner, berated her. I could see peeking out from underneath their serious demeanor they were one step away from uncontrollable laughter.

Sometimes their friends were included, and even toddlers were dressed up and given detailed direction about their performance. Much to the chagrin of the girls, if their friends' enthusiasm waned because the production went on too long, they would conjure up all of their persuasive skills to convince the friends to keep going; most of the time it worked. Some of the funniest moments we have recorded on film were not from written lines, but from Charlotte and Vanessa being caught on camera in the process of this persuasion, forgetting to turn off the camera amidst all the confusion. The film was saved because they rarely edited their work; they were too busy moving on to the next project.

At the age of thirteen they were still making videos, only now these consisted of them singing songs, doing fashion shows, and giving tours of the house and farm. Basically they were videotaping scenes from their everyday lives.

In one film, a classic twin rivalry reveals itself when Vanessa is conducting a tour of the living room. She picks up one of the Valentine cards they had made for us and starts reciting the verse. After putting the card back on the table, she begins singing *Somewhere Over the Rainbow*. Meanwhile, Charlotte is behind the camera filming, but most important, out of the limelight. The next moment, Charlotte is sideling up to Vanessa, having placed the camera on a tripod, not missing a beat while joining in the song.

All the while they are singing and smiling for the camera, you can see slight nudges, each one trying to be in full view of the camera. After singing one more song, Vanessa says to Charlotte in the sweetest voice possible, "Well, I think it's time for you to go back behind the camera." Charlotte, clearly trying to look unperturbed in front of the camera's all-seeing eye, says "okay" with a big smile. But as she moves away, ever so slightly she gives one last little nudge, hoping it will not be seen, while Vanessa happily starts in with another song, clearly pleased to be the center of attention again.

Some of these revealing ad lib videos would end with them falling on the floor, cracking each other up over the silliest of things, and the laughter would undoubtedly provoke a coughing attack. It's funny, but I don't often think of all of the coughing back then, but watching these videos brings it all back.

"We get tickle torture to get the green meanies out," Vanessa would explain, as they would try to continue talking through these coughing episodes, making jokes about the "green meanies" that lived within their bodies. Actually, we did tickle them to make them cough when they were little, after clapping their chests to loosen the mucus in their lungs. They liked the tickling much better than the clapping therapy and many times it worked, loosening up what was deep in the recesses of their lungs. It was interesting to hear them talk about why they were coughing and how it affected them and made me again realize just how aware they were of their illness at such a young age.

When the girls reached junior high school, acting in the school play was the highlight of their year. But they also continued with their piano lessons and they played in the band; Vanessa on flute and Charlotte on the clarinet, and they sang in the chorus. Basically they did anything that meant they could be in the limelight on stage.

Chapter 13

Charlotte, Vanessa

"I always knew I had CF because we did chest pt. My parents pounded my chest to break up the mucus so we could cough it out, so we always knew we had this different thing and it wasn't good but I also knew that all cases were different. I thought we were a pretty good case, since we were never sick. The first time I realized was when there was a documentary about a girl named Alex, who dies when she is eight years old from CF. I went to a friend's house and she showed me the movie about the girl who died and I can remember seeing in the movie how she coughed up blood right before she died. That didn't bother me until her mom came home and her mom was furious that my friend had showed me this movie. It made me think that she knew something that I didn't know."

Charlotte

"It's funny, looking back as a child I thought CF made me special, not different. When I was young, I was never told of its long-term fatal effects and thought my regular hospital visits were normal and every child had them. I remember as a child I would tell people with a proud smile, "I am a twin and have CF!" It's funny how children see things. Hospital stays were full of gifts, balloons and flowers, which made me

feel special. It was not until the sixth grade that my eyes were rudely opened and my attitude severely altered.

"I was asked by a close friend to explain what CF was. I tried my best but found it hard to fully explain. So when I got home, I went into our household library and pulled down a large black dusty book marked, "Medical Illnesses". I sifted through its fragile pages located cystic fibrosis and began reading the finely printed column. It explained the reason for our thick mucus and the ailments associated with it. I read on, nothing new, until the end where I learned that cystic fibrosis is the number one genetic killer of children, claiming thousands before their tenth birthdays. "Tenth" and "fatal" thundered over and over in my brain. I read the article again and again and again, hoping that maybe I'd read it wrong or maybe it was the wrong column. I did not. I crammed the heavy book back into its proper place and ran to my room to cry. I never told anyone about it for fear that hearing the words out loud would make it a steadfast reality.

"I kept this knowledge to myself until my next hospital visit when I asked my doctor about what I had read. He confirmed my fear but said the article was old, and with new medication and therapy the average life span was eighteen. I pushed this information to the back of my mind; I was not sick; I was not going to die.

"Things again were good and I managed to get on with my life until the summer before seventh grade. My family and I had taken a trip to California to visit my Aunt Janice and cousin Josh in Sausalito. Her apartment complex had a pool and Jacuzzi. Being that my sister and I were fish, we spent most of our time in the pool. It was the third day and as usual, Charlotte and I had spent a good three or four hours running back and forth from the steaming Jacuzzi to the sparkling pool. While absorbing the bubbles, I coughed, not an unusual act, yet when I looked down my hand was filled with specks of blood. Blood. I quickly dipped my hand in the water, not wanting to alarm my sister, and continued to play as normally as possible.

"Becoming prunes, we headed back to the condo. I kept my secret well and proceeded to take my shower. I finished and began drying myself off when I coughed again, this time into the sink. I looked down, shocked at the crimson sprayed all over the white porcelain. I guess my mother noticed my face as she passed the bathroom. She looked at me and then followed my glance toward the sink and immediately met my eyes once more. I remember this moment well for it was the first time I

58

saw my mother actually show fear, and the first time I confronted her with mine. I remember my exact words, 'Am I going to die now?'

"My mom replied no but I heard the lack of sureness in her words and saw the restrained tears shining within the corners of her eyes. How could I be coughing up blood, being as healthy as I was?

"It turned out to be a nosebleed running down my throat, but the overall effect changed my life. For the first time I accepted my fate, and tried to funnel all the energy I had spent worrying about the future into more positive issues, for instance, my goal to become an actress.

"Things went well until eighth grade. My sister fell ill on our fourteenth birthday. I remember crying a lot, not only for her, but also for us. I thought, "Hey, I'm fourteen and already well over half of eighteen, over half of my life is over." Charlotte became healthier and was released, but things were somehow different. I remember how she spoke of children with CF dying down the hall in the hospital, children younger than we were. She spoke of a child's nightlong cries and his release before Christmas for fear he would not make it. They wanted him to spend the short time he had, united with his family. In the next two years, I thought a lot about death."

Vanessa

The moment Vanessa coughed up that sink full of blood in California a tiny wound opened in my heart and continued to grow. I was forced to realize once again how fragile our life really was and would continue to be.

Chapter 14

Vanessa, Charlotte

"You should always go for what you want to go for, so that you don't sit there and think 'I wish I had done that or tried this'—even if it doesn't work out at least you would have tried it. I would sit down and look at my life and say, Listen, I could sit here and be miserable and depressed and say I have been given a bad rap, but everyone, some way or another, is given a bad rap. You have to look at the positives in your life and focus on that and that helps me move on."

Vanessa

In the summer of 1986, things started changing on the farm. My dad had died in June after his long, silent battle with cancer and Mr. Keenan, the owner of the farm and the horse business, was sending us signals we could not quite decipher. For the next four years, we lived in a deteriorating situation, asking constant questions about what our future would be on the farm, but never getting any real answers. For years we had been living on a very small salary, with nothing left over to save, leaving us in a very precarious situation with few options. And now, our future depended on a man whose strange behavior and ominous control over our lives was coming to light.

Through the summer of 1989, the situation only grew worse. Months of meetings resulted in far more questions with no answers until one day after a six hour meeting, Jeff was fired. He had pressed too hard for information about his pension.

It was the beginning of September and the girls had just started their last year of junior high school. We could not leave at this time. We had no home, no job, no savings, not even unemployment insurance because of a loophole in the system that Mr. Keenan took advantage of.

Thankfully, Rich Caruso, one of the partners in the horse business and a longtime friend, arranged for Jeff to speak to a lawyer in a large Philadelphia law firm to see if they could help us. The case was taken on a contingency basis with a $5,000 retaining fee. Rich paid the fee and we finally had a voice. It would take five years for us to be heard in federal court and another year after winning the case to get a settlement, which finally enabled us to repay Rich for his kindness.

The first thing we did was to file in local court to be able to remain in the house until Jeff found a job and a place to live. He continued working with the horses and taking care of the property without salary so we could stay on. The house we needed to find had to be big enough to also accommodate my mom, since she had spent most of her life savings fixing up the spring house and Mr. Keenan now denied all the of promises he had made to my father and her.

Jeff knew we would have to move to Kentucky for him to stay in the horse business. The doctors advised against it because there were no CF centers in the area at the time, so Jeff started looking for any other type of job that would provide good health insurance for the girls. It was not an easy process. Jeff was forty-four and had never worked in a corporation and it was a time when jobs were scarce. He sent out many resumes, never hearing back from anyone.

Finally, in November, a friend and neighbor secured an interview for Jeff and he was hired. We will always be grateful for our friend's kindness.

In January 1990, Jeff started at ARCO Chemical Company. Although it was a far cry from the horse business, it gave us a future to build on. At the end of February, we found a twin house in Phoenixville, Pennsylvania, which we purchased with a VA loan.

◈◈

We endured Mr. Keenan's daily intrusions and bizarre behavior until we packed our last box into the car and drove from the farm, never looking back. It was the first time I didn't cry or walk through the empty house to say thank you for all the good memories we had shared. The pain was too much. All we wanted to do was escape.

It is strange, the things you remember from very stressful times. Luckily, you can't really conjure up the pain, but you do remember moments that will never fade with time. This was one of many.

For their thirteenth birthday, Charlotte and Vanessa both had wanted waterbeds. Not just any waterbeds, but the big ornate ones with a built-in mirror and bookcases in the headboard. So for their birthday, we packed away their twin beds and surprised Charlotte with her queen waterbed and Vanessa with her oversized twin, since she now had the smaller room. They loved these beds, so warm and toasty in the winter as they crawled in-between the sheets at night. Their friends loved coming over for the night to sleep on the warm waves lulling them to sleep. Charlotte was especially enamored with hers.

But the rooms were much smaller in the house we were moving to. The bedrooms on the second floor would never support the size or weight of these beds. When we told Charlotte her bed wouldn't fit in her new room, she started to cry. "Please don't make me give up my bed."

We felt utterly miserable, but we had to sell both beds in order to pay for the new ones to fit into their smaller rooms. We put an ad in the paper and they sold immediately. The day came to drain the beds; the couple was coming to pick them up. I went upstairs and Charlotte would not get off her bed. She was crying and through the tears kept asking us not to take the bed away. I will never forget her face; it is just one of the many disturbing memories I have from this sad period in our lives.

◈◈

It took five long years before we went to court and won the case against him. There was absolutely no satisfaction in winning, but was a necessity to move forward in our lives. I learned from going to court that you can tell the truth and it doesn't matter; it isn't heard. The experience was nauseating—and we won, if that can be called winning. The headline in one of the papers read, "Court Rules Against Feudal Lord...." We were awarded $120,000, with the stipulation that we drop the charges pertaining to the pension, the stronger case and the heart of the lawsuit. At this point, we were exhausted from it all and decided it was too much stress in our lives to continue fighting. We needed to find peace again and we cried uncle; money never has nor ever will be the focus of our lives.

The lawyer took 60 percent. The rest was used to pay bills. Finally, closure came to that part of our life, but it left us beaten in the process. Mr. Keenan finally had been wiped from our lives, but the girls' illness was waiting in the wings.

Living under these conditions with the stress mounting all around us, the girls began to get sick. Hospitalizations increased.

One reason not to be in the hospital became evident to us only when it was too late. Charlotte was again hospitalized when we heard from the nurses that they were thinking of quarantining cystic fibrosis patients who tested positive for pseudomonas cepacia, a bacteria resistant to all antibiotics and especially dangerous to cystic fibrosis patients.

There was a four-year old girl down the hall from Charlotte who rarely had visitors. She tested positive for the bacteria. She would come into Charlotte's room and climb all over her and although we constantly reminded Charlotte about the risk, she did not have the heart to tell the girl to leave when we were not there. That was pure Charlotte; she was more worried about the little girl who needed company than she was about herself.

During that hospital visit, Charlotte contracted pseudomonas cepacia, which later in life cost her the chance for a lung transplant. Vanessa contracted it a few months later, most likely from Charlotte. The policy for quarantine became mandatory shortly after Charlotte's stay. We all suffered from this move away from the farm. But it was the girls who suffered most because their health took a huge toll as they dealt with the harsh reality of their new world and the world to come.

The sadness began settling in.

Chapter 15

Vanessa, Jeff, Charlotte, Pat

"My life has not been without its hills and bumps. Not wanting people to know about my cystic fibrosis, keeping it a secret while growing up because I didn't want to be different, was difficult. When I was about to go through the important transition from ninth to tenth grade, my life was thrown into disarray. My father lost his job and we were forced to leave the safety of the farm, my home. With limited choices, my family moved to Phoenixville, a small town outside of Valley Forge Park, which was once a thriving steel mill town. The mill was closed ten years ago, resulting in troubled times for many of the families who live here. Many students came from broken homes and unstable environments. Although I was very disappointed by losing my old friends, I was hoping to make new friends with whom I could share new experiences. At that time, I had absolutely no idea that these experiences would force me to grow up so quickly.

"Being new in a small school, my sister and I became the main attraction. My tenth grade year was an extremely stressful, confusing and sad time for me, having to make difficult choices I was not ready to make. Most of these people smoked and drank, two acts I very briefly experimented with, participating because I wanted to be accepted. To avoid the pressure, I would say the smoke affected my cystic fibrosis or the alcohol would cause an allergic reaction with my current medications. I was scared and very unhappy in my new life, as if I was trapped and alone in a world I could not escape from.

"This was not me, it was someone else. Throughout tenth grade, I struggled. I could not understand why life was worth living when I knew I would eventually become sick and die a slow death; a death in which my mind and soul would want to live, yet my body would be fading away."

Charlotte

*I*n June of 1990, with my mom in tow, we moved a mere six miles away. For Charlotte and Vanessa, it was a million miles from home. There were no raspberry bushes, there were no woods to walk in, no flaming trees under our windows to mark the passing of the seasons. But it was a place to begin again and we were grateful for that.

The move from Chester Springs, a land of rolling hills, open spaces and private lives, to Phoenixville, a town which at that time had seen better days, was not an easy one. The street we lived on was one of the nicer ones in town. The house was a one hundred-year-old brick twin. Our neighbors were friendly, although they lived much closer to us than we were used to.

The night before we left the farm, I dug up a small piece of the lilac bush the girls had given me. I wanted to take the whole line of bushes, but the roots of a lilac run deep and strong and it was impossible to dig them up. We chose a sunny spot in the small backyard of our new home, hoping it would take. The next year, it bloomed profusely, growing tall and full, enough to share cuttings with our neighbors.

Jeff was working away from home now and I was finishing my degree. Initially, when the situation began to deteriorate, I was going to look for a job right away, but Jeff convinced me to finish school, especially with only a few classes left. I also worked part time and received a student loan to help pay for the extras. Graduating with a BA, Summa Cum Laude, in the spring of 1991 was an important step for me. I was the first in my family to go to college, as Jeff was in his. The opportunities afforded to me because of my degree leave me forever grateful that I didn't give up. Staying in school also provided something positive in my life when all else was falling apart. It was an important lesson not to change course when all signs pointed otherwise.

We were all overwhelmed by this new life, but none more than Charlotte and Vanessa. The girls were used to our being there all the time and now we couldn't be. As soon as I completed my degree, I needed to work full time to help support our family. But this only added to the stress of everyone trying to cope with these new circumstances. The girls barely left the house the entire summer. They were in shock from this dramatic change in their lives.

The first day of school arrived. I will never forget coming home from work, opening the front door and seeing six boys in the living room, with no sign of Charlotte or Vanessa. I found them alone upstairs in their rooms. They seemed anxious as they described to me how these boys had followed them home from school and just came in the house and made themselves comfortable, with no invitation.

I suddenly realized that all through their life at the farm, we always brought their friends to our house; no one just walked over, it was too far. They had no experience in this new environment; they didn't know where the boundaries were and how to express them if they did exist. We had all lived in innocent isolation; this was a whole new set of rules. They were suddenly thrust into situations we hadn't prepared them for. Their childhood and innocence had ended abruptly, without a trace.

Chapter 16

"A Portrait Poem"

A reflection of myself

Gleaming, curly, flowing, blond hair

Her brownish-gold eyes resemble an autumn leaf

As her features hold a classic

But distraught look

Her lean body portrays elegance and beauty

She is gay and joyous

Always flashing a ready smile,

Even on the worst of days,

She brings out the best in everyone.

Yet I dislike the fact that she, my twin sister,

Places a mask over which she acts out life like a play,

Yet deep down she is someone quite different.

A tiny, frightened, innocent girl

Filled with a quaint charm and wittiness.

Charlotte and I are quite different, both physically

And mentally, yet at crucial times we are drawn together in the tightest of bonds.

As for my sister, we'll lean on each other for strength and guidance for fate is what you make it and we, the strong willed, will survive."

Vanessa

*I*n their new school, Charlotte and Vanessa quickly became the center of attraction, something they did not want or ask for in this new environment. This was a small town and most of the kids had grown up in a very circumscribed world. Being a twin is fascinating to many people and especially when the girls were so friendly and outgoing. Therefore, on the first day of school they assumed they could be friendly to everyone. They quickly realized it just didn't work that way here.

Many of the students were at school because that was where they had to be at this particular juncture in their lives, not where they wanted to be. Charlotte and Vanessa did not fit into any one particular group. The rougher kids, whom the girls had never really had encounters with before, harassed them in the hall and after school, the boys sometimes purposely bumping into them trying to touch them. Vanessa went to the principal and complained; she hardened with the pressure, while Charlotte grew afraid.

It seemed that year there was one crisis after another and we soon sought psychiatric counseling to cope with the deteriorating situation at home. I remember our first visit. The psychiatrist said that just one of the life changes that had happened to us in the past year was enough to throw a family over the edge, never mind seven or eight changes. We were trying to cope with too much. The violent move from the farm, the loss of Jeff's job and coping with the corporate world, me working to help pay the bills and not being there all the time, the girls' illness, the death of Jeff's mother from cancer the year we moved, and my mother living in the same small house with us. We were all overwhelmed.

He told us that just being a twin was a stressful situation, never mind all the rest. The girls saw him for over a year; Jeff and I sat in occasionally. It was a long journey, but with his help and the passage of time, our family began to heal.

School was another matter. It took the entire first year and many conferences to work out the issues involving aggressive kids who would not leave the girls alone. Every day it was a fight to get them to go school at all, and they had always excelled in school. English class and the school play were the only positives during the entire first year. The strain was showing on all of us. But thankfully, as summer approached, things began calming down.

By the time they were ready to go back to school in the fall, they were looking forward to their junior year and had their sights set on going to college. We thought all the problems that had plagued their sophomore year were finally worked out, but we were wrong; there was still one more confrontation to go.

As they walked home from school that first day of junior year, three of the girls who had threatened them the year before, menacingly slipped into step with them five blocks from home. They told Charlotte and Vanessa that they were going to beat them up. Their hateful intimidation continued all the way home.

As soon as I came through the front door after work, Charlotte jumped off the sofa and through her tears and frightened eyes said she would never go back to school, ever again. Vanessa stood behind Charlotte allowing her say it for both of them. Something snapped in me.

All the work we had done over the past year was wiped away in the girls' terrifying walk home. Jeff came home after me and I grabbed his arm. "We are going to those girls' houses. We are not going back to start this all over again this year."

At all three apartments, we explained to each parent what had happened that afternoon and asked to speak to their daughter. When each one came out of her room, face to face we told them that if the girls were threatened or harmed in any way ever again, we would have the police at their door and would make sure that charges were filed. We had had enough. It was over.

As we drove home from the last apartment, I was shaking with anger and frustration that it had come to this. Why did there have to be all this meanness in the world? Wasn't life hard enough?

Chapter 17

Charlotte, Vanessa

"What is living without relationships? You have to have relationships, but now what I did to protect myself was when I would get into a relationship, I would always start out by laying it on the line and saying, Look, I have cystic fibrosis, I may die, do you still want to be my friend? And then I would take it from there. I wanted to warn people because it's not fair to get into a relationship and get close to someone and not be honest, so that is how I dealt with making new friends now."

Vanessa

Vanessa dealt with the situation differently. She didn't care as much if people didn't like her. She was not going to change who she was and this helped to quell her fear of not being accepted. The pressure and fear Charlotte felt was processed as anger for Vanessa and in this way she became stronger and charged ahead in the way that only Vanessa could.

For the next two years, Charlotte and Vanessa focused their lives around school plays, musicals, writing and joining the local theater group, things they felt passionate about. Vanessa excelled at character acting, sometimes taking on several roles in one play. She also carried her characters into life. For her senior prom, she dressed up like Audrey Hepburn from *Breakfast at Tiffany's* and insisted her date wear a top hat and cane.

There were many times I was stopped around town to hear accolades about a particular performance. "Vanessa was so believable as Yenta in *Fiddler on the Roof*. I never would have known it was her beneath the makeup; what a character." Or "Vanessa was made for the part of Reno Sweeney in *Anything Goes*. She sure can belt out those numbers." The funny thing was, she never could dance, but they accommodated for that. She would start the number with a little dance and then would say, "Take it away girls," while stepping aside and it worked. Charlotte had the lead in *The Paper Chase*, and she received a standing ovation when she sang "On My Own" from the musical *Les Miserables*. They were in their glory when they were on stage and in the spotlight.

They found their enthusiasm for school again. Their teachers told me they were always ready to raise their hand and participate in discussions, which the teachers found refreshing. The girls actually had more contact with the teachers than the students at this point and they liked it that way. English class, especially writing, became their favorite class, with art a close second. Paintings, ceramic cups, boxes, wooden candleholders, and a vast array of other little creations, they made all of these. I reflected that they had inherited my father's gift of working with his hands.

߂ℓ߂

Our life was finally settling down into some semblance of normalcy, whatever that was at this point, so I was in complete shock when one bitter cold Monday morning in January, I started to cry. On my way to work at the Atwater Kent museum, riding the R-5, a packed commuter train to Philadelphia, I was in my usual seat looking out the window reading the paper, when all of a sudden it started. It took me totally by surprise, and worse, I couldn't stop. I suppose all the losses and not sleeping well for two years had eroded into my soul. I rode the forty-five minutes into the city, my face to the window, trying to conceal the tears running down my face. I didn't know what to do when I got off the train in the city at the 30th Street Station, so I quickly crossed the platform and rode another sixty minutes back out, straight to our HMO physician, whom I had never visited before.

"Why didn't you come sooner?" he asked, when I told him what had happened.

"I thought I could make it, keep going, stay strong," was my tired reply.

When I think back to this time in our life, it conjures up so many emotions. We were all so angry at something we had no control over, both losing the life we once had, and starting to see the signs of living everyday with a chronic illness. I was drowning in so many emotions, trying desperately to keep my head above water, while every new ripple sent me deeper, gasping for air. Concealing it well for a long time had finally taken its toll.

My doctor prescribed an anti-depressant and an anti-anxiety drug, which he said should allow me to sleep. That night I slept through most of the night for the first time in years. I took the anti-anxiety drug for a few weeks and the anti-depressant for at least nine months and vowed never again to let myself slip that deeply into sadness without asking for help.

Our life had finally settled into a routine as we came to enjoy our newfound peace. We tried to enjoy our days together as the girls looked forward to their future.

Chapter 18

Charlotte

"It took over a year for me to realize that if I were to ever like myself again, I would have to change back to who I was and be true to myself. Slowly, I broke away from these people and began to do things that made me feel better about myself. I reunited with old friends who did not pressure me to do things I did not want to do. I realized I had my whole life in front of me and there were many opportunities just waiting to be seized. I was ready to move on to college and to form trusting relationships that would continue for the rest of my life."

Charlotte

*L*earning to drive changed Charlotte's life. When she turned sixteen, all she wanted was her driving permit. She considered this her ticket to freedom, giving her the chance to visit her old friends, since they lived more than twenty miles away and we couldn't take her over there as much as she wanted.

Both Charlotte and Vanessa had driven the red pickup truck around the farm with Jeff when they were about fourteen, so they had been behind the wheel before, although the truck was a challenge to drive since it was a stick shift and did not have power steering or power brakes. One day Jeff was letting them drive and Charlotte got a little too close to the barn and couldn't stop fast enough, adding one more dent to its hide.

ॐ

When Charlotte received her permit and eased herself behind the wheel for the first time, she automatically put her seat belt on, adjusted the mirrors, looked into the side view mirror and pulled out from the curve, never looking back. We knew right away she was a natural born driver, and she received her license in one try. In her second year of college, we bought her a used Saab with a stick shift. My brother-in-law, Ross, took her out to teach her to drive the manual transmission in of all places, the streets and hills of San Francisco. She grasped the technique in twenty minutes.

As soon as Charlotte received her license, she spent most weekends driving to see her old friends in Downingtown. One evening, late at night, she came in the door crying and shaking. When we were able to finally calm her down, she sobbed, "I was driving on Route 113, close to the farm and something ran out into the road and I hit it. I pulled off the road and ran back to see what it was. Mom, it was a baby fawn. She was just lying there on the side of the road so I sat down and pulled her onto my lap and stayed with her until she died. Her mom was standing behind me in the bushes, next to Hallman's field. "Mom, I killed Bambi."

We all went over and buried the fawn, but Charlotte, the lover of all animals, especially those who were hurt or in trouble, would always remember that night as the night she killed Bambi.

ॐ

When it came to Vanessa driving, it was a whole different story. First, she didn't ask to get her permit until she was eighteen. She didn't have the intense need to go back to see her old friends like Charlotte did and besides, she had Charlotte to drive her around. She learned the basics quickly when she did obtain her permit, but our first excursion down a winding country road was alarming.

It was early evening and Vanessa said she wanted to try out her new wings. We piled into our huge Country Squire station wagon, blue

78

with fake wood trim, with Vanessa at the wheel, me in the front seat and Jeff in the back. After leaving the town of Phoenixville, we turned onto Route 29, a six-mile stretch of road known for its curves and narrow bridges over the Pickering Creek, with very little traffic. Vanessa started speeding up.

"Vanessa, aren't you going a little fast for this road?" I asked. "No," she said, turning to look at me. "I'm doing the speed limit," she continued, still looking at me instead of at the road. I put my hand on the dashboard bracing myself as we flew over the narrow bridge. "Vanessa, I think you just clipped that bridge, slow down," I said, a little too loud. "I didn't hit the bridge," she fired back as she sped into the next curve, her eyes again on me, not the road.

We asked her to slow down and keep her eyes on the road. There was no shoulder on which to pull over, so we had no choice but to continue on. As she slowed down, a car passed us in a no passing zone, just missing a car coming over the hill on the opposite side of the road. Vanessa had to swerve to miss the car, which veered into our lane. By the time we got to the mall, the ten miles there seemed like fifty. On the way back, Jeff drove. Even years later when we would joke about her first big driving experience, Vanessa still would never admit she had hit that bridge.

During the next few weeks, Jeff took Vanessa out driving a few more times, minus the mom, when she suddenly decided she was ready to take her driving test. We thought for sure she would not pass the test on her first attempt, so we decided to let her give it a try.

When we arrived for the test, the person at the desk told Vanessa, "Last week we made parallel parking a requirement again. It was dropped for several years, but we added it last week so if you haven't practiced, it's probably a waste of time for you to take the test." Although Vanessa had never really practiced parallel parking, she was not one to back down from a challenge. "Oh, I'll just go and take the test; what the heck."

Jeff and I looked at each other when Vanessa went to get in line for her test. Jeff said what I was thinking. "This is the perfect excuse. When she doesn't pass, she won't feel so bad."

Vanessa waited for her turn and we smiled when she drove off with the instructor. We watched it all from a distance. When she came to the orange cones to parallel park, she pulled up beside the front one, turned her wheel and backed in perfectly between the two cones just enough before she eased the car forward a tad and stopped. The car sat equidistant between the two cones. Jeff and I just looked at one another, dumbstruck.

When the test was finished and they pulled up to the curb, Vanessa was smiling. "I haven't had anyone in the past week parallel park as well as she just did," the officer said, shaking his head. I must admit all Jeff and I were thinking was how nervous we were, knowing she would be on the road driving; parallel parking was one thing, driving another.

Actually, she turned out to be a safe but somewhat distracted driver, tending to drive slowly on highways and fast on small narrow roads, a habit she never changed. What's funny is that she remained truly awesome at parallel parking. Whenever Vanessa had a tight space, she would slide that car in with one try, and a little satisfied smile would spread across her face.

Chapter 19

Vanessa

"Don"
In this world it's rare to find,
A man so giving, a man so kind,
A man whose heart is full of love,
Matched with a soul from far above.
When I am down he makes me smile,
With positive words, I laugh with style.
He always finds the good in all,
He picks you up when you fall.
And despite his hardships he's always there,
He overcomes his pain to provide our care.
He gives and gives till all is gone,
This special person is a man named Don.
He touched our family though words cannot show,
He helped us heal; he helped us grow.
He gave us a gift, which never ends,
He let us in and made us friends.
Thank you Don for all you've done,
If we were the moon, you'd be our sun.
For it's never dark when you are there,

In April of 1992, Charlotte was invited to go to the junior prom at her old high school. This was very important to her. We bought a short, black silk dress and were all set for the big night. Then, the week before, she started with a fever and her coughing increased. After seeing her doctor, he confirmed she had another lung infection. Charlotte reluctantly agreed to be admitted to the hospital, but not without some concessions, the first that she be able to get a pass to go to the prom. The pass was only good for six hours, any longer would greatly impact her antibiotic schedule, so it would take a lot of juggling but it was workable.

The day of the prom, I brought everything to the hospital so she could get dressed. Since I had to pick up Dave, her date, the nurses agreed to help get her dressed, which included pulling her intravenous pick line for the six hours she would be away. Crazy, I know, but we do what we have to.

I came back with Dave. Mind you, it is more than an hour trip to Downingtown and back, and when I returned to the hospital and opened the door to Charlotte's room, everyone was having a nervous breakdown.

Her dress, which fit her perfectly when we bought it, would not fit around her chest now because the infection in her lungs had caused her rib cage to expand from the trapped air. Consequently, they could not zip up the dress.

They tried every way imaginable, including putting clamp scissors on the zipper with Charlotte on her stomach across the bed, trying not to breathe. Needless to say, the zipper would not budge, but the scissors slipped and hit the nurse in the nose, luckily it wasn't her eye. Finally after all the tears and not knowing what else to do, I turned down the remaining part of the dress to the half closed zipper and made the back into a V. What can I say, we were desperate, but it worked.

We all finally jumped in the car and drove to the dance. At the agreed upon hour, I picked them up and took her back to the hospital, a little late, but happy.

৵৻

The stress of the move and all that followed meant that the girls' times at the hospital grew more frequent for "tune-ups". That usually involved two to four weeks of intravenous antibiotics and intensive physical therapy, needed for the constant infections now in their lungs and the growing resistance to antibiotics. Since hospital stays were long and sleep deprived, when we heard about home care, we jumped at the chance to try it.

This time, the girls were in the hospital together and after several weeks it was decided they could continue their intravenous antibiotics and respiratory treatments at home. Homecare, which was just getting started, was new to everyone, including the staff at the hospital, but it meant the girls would get more sleep, eat better and not be exposed to the growing problem of hospital resistant germs.

Since this was the first time and we had to make arrangements for two, it took several days to coordinate everything between the insurance company and the home care agency.

After their two weeks in the hospital, I packed up all their things, and it amounted to a great deal of stuff. I signed and delivered all the discharge forms to the office downstairs and spoke to the nurses and doctors about their new routine at home. All their prescriptions, both new and old, were discussed and written at this time, so I could drop them off at the pharmacy on the way home. This could easily be up to twenty prescriptions and I didn't want to forget any.

The routine always took longer than anticipated and it wasn't until the middle of the afternoon and several trips up and down on the elevator that I finally finished packing the car and settled the girls in the back seat for the hour-long drive home.

৵৻

The homecare nurse arrived at the house ten minutes after we did, so we didn't get a chance to catch our breath. It took him awhile to get all the equipment and medicines into the house and separated into piles for each of the girls, with the IV poles coming through the door last. He then took a moment to catch his breath.

Since their next intravenous antibiotic was due, he asked Charlotte and Vanessa to sit down on the couch so he could go over the procedure with them and get them started before he and I did the hours of paperwork; like I said all of this was new. I sat across the room and watched.

As he set up the IV poles, I heard Vanessa say, "Why doesn't the IV pole have the monitor attached that pumps in the medicine?" He was busy getting the tubing untangled so it took him a few minutes to answer. "The insurance company won't pay for the monitor so you will be using the gravity fed type of infusion."

"Oh," was all they said, but I could see they were concerned.

To complicate matters, Charlotte had come home with a PIC line in her arm. After several tries in the hospital to find a vein for a peripheral intravenous line, Charlotte had to sadly admit it was time to get a pick line. This happens when the veins have either collapsed or are so scarred by the harsh antibiotics that a regular peripheral line lasts only a few hours before failing.

A pick line is a long, thin, flexible tube inserted into a vein through an incision generally between the wrist and elbow, and carefully threaded up the arm and around the armpit where it empties into a larger vein in the upper chest. The tube is stitched at the incision and covered with sterile bandages, leaving an access line for the medicine to be hooked up to. When the course of treatment is over, the line is pulled to prevent infection, which could be very serious because it is so close to the heart.

On top of all of this, both the girls were allergic to all tape, breaking out with large blisters unless special bandages were used. These were only available at the hospital. Luckily, I had asked the nurses for a few of the bandages before we left because the request hadn't been relayed to the homecare company and he didn't have any to redress their IV lines. In the scheme of things, it wasn't a big deal, only one more thing to think about.

It was warm in the room when we got home so I turned on the air conditioner when beads of sweat began popping out on the nurse's forehead. He was standing about four feet in front of the girls, who were seated on the couch, as he hung a bag of medicine on the pole and said again, "This is a gravity fed method of infusion so no monitor is required." I saw the girls look at each other.

He continued going through the steps, showing us how to attach the tubing to the bag of medicine, open the clamp to allow the medicine to flow down the tubing to the end where it dripped into a paper cup so he could count the drops for the correct dosage. By adjusting the height of the IV pole, the rate of drops coming through changed, the higher the pole, the faster the drops. All the while, the girls continued to watch and listen. Finally, after counting the drops and adjusting the pole numerous times to get the correct dosage, he clamped off the flow of medicine by turning the little wheel in the opposite direction.

By now, he was sweating profusely. It had taken such a long time to get the drops to drip at the right speed, he was getting nervous. As he cleaned and inserted the tubing into their IV line, he said they would need to count the drops again after it was attached to make sure the line was still releasing the same amount of medicine per minute.

All through this very long process, the girls looked attentive, but they were absolutely quiet, which was very unusual for them. When he was finished, Charlotte asked, "Since I have a PIC line, will it take longer than forty-five minutes to finish the first medicine, since you know we have another antibiotic to do after that?"

"Gravity fed IV's are slower than monitor fed systems and it could take even longer with a PIC line," answered the nurse. The girls looked at each other again.

"Well, then we're not going to do it. Why can't we get a monitor for the pole or better yet, get the IV's the nurses told us about that look like hand grenades and are small enough to fit in your pocket so you can move around without the pole?"

"Well, the insurance company will only pay for the gravity fed system at home so that's what was ordered," he replied.

A few moments passed before Charlotte said, "Then we're going back into the hospital because this is way too much work and it's so slow we won't be able to do anything except sit on the couch attached to the IV poles day and night." I just sat back and watched.

Armed with the knowledge that there were much simpler methods available, Charlotte and Vanessa refused to accept the system. The questions kept flying and he kept sweating as he spoke. "The insurance company will not change their mind on this. It's a waste of time to try." The girls were always up for a challenge and this was a big one. "Do you have the telephone number for the insurance company?" Charlotte asked. He gave her the number and she immediately got up off the couch and dialed. I was amazed at their determination to do what was right.

I could hear Charlotte on the phone in the kitchen explaining the situation in a very clear and concise manner. "I know of several different methods of infusion and they are all better than this gravity fed method. If you can't make it easier for us to stay at home for the rest of our treatments, then we'll both go back into the hospital tonight and that would cost the insurance company more money."

This went on for about twenty minutes, back and forth, with lots of on-hold time. The next thing we knew, Charlotte came in and said to the nurse, "they want to speak to you." He went into the kitchen and picked up the phone. When he came back out a few minutes later, he started packing up all the equipment saying he was taking it back and that he would return later in the evening with the small, portable IV's. He said he was shocked because the insurance company had never done that before and he was impressed.

I was so proud. The girls had won their first battle with the insurance company and believe me, it is a battle with those companies when you are sick in this country.

With this easier method, I could take their medicines out of the refrigerator to warm up a few hours before their infusion and easily attach it to their lines without waking them during the night. Their antibiotics took at least one hour to infuse and were administered back-to-back every six hours so there was always a dose in the middle of the night. Each antibiotic required the IV to be flushed with saline before and after each dose so it was a rigorous routine when they were receiving three antibiotics consecutively, but it still made our lives easier. And most of all they could sleep in their own beds.

※※

This first home care experience brought Don, the girls' respiratory therapist, into our lives. He was one of the most caring individuals we have ever met. While dealing with his own illness, multiple sclerosis, he would drive an hour each way to our home, sometimes three times a day, to do their therapy.

Years later, I found out that many of these visits were never reimbursed by the insurance company, but he still came. On his many visits, he not only dealt with Charlotte and Vanessa's physical needs, he became their friend and confidant, which sometimes was even more important. He truly listened to their fears and was able to talk to them freely and honestly about life and death.

Don was able to deal with all the emotional ups and downs, providing a lifeline to Charlotte and Vanessa and to me, when we desperately needed one. He was a gift to our family and we will always be grateful to him.

Chapter 20

Darius, Vanessa

"Darius and I have been together for eight years now. I guess I met him when I was a junior, going into the eleventh grade. I came out to visit my Aunt Janice in Sausalito and met Darius. We dated on and off long distance for a while. I loved the theater and knew California was the place to be ever since the day I first stepped off the plane. That was when I was in fifth grade and we were on vacation there. I said 'I'm going to school out here to Santa Barbara or San Diego.' Then I met Darius and it was history. I said, "Mom and Dad, I really am going to go to school out there."

Vanessa

L ove entered Vanessa's life in the summer of 1990; she was sixteen years old. It was Vanessa and Charlotte's second trip to California and they were staying with my sister Jan for a few weeks in Sausalito, across the bay from San Francisco. During that visit, Vanessa met Darius, a friend and fellow surfer of my sister's son, Josh.

From that day on, her life changed. Darius would become the love of Vanessa's life. The letters and phone calls began when she returned home and they never stopped. Darius came to visit us several times in Pennsylvania, and Vanessa in turn visited him in California. It was a long distance relationship, but that certainly did not dampen the intensity of their love.

From the time she met Darius, she never wavered in her love for him. All through high school, boys would come over to visit. They would sit on the couch in the living room and I could see they were smitten with her, but Vanessa either didn't see their attentions or chose to ignore them. Whatever the reason, her conversation invariably turned to Darius, much to their chagrin.

Eventually, they were satisfied to be her friend and Darius remained her one and only until the day she died.

> *"Darius"*
> *You are the one who made me forget the world*
> *Your smile is sunshine*
> *Your touch a warm breeze*
> *Your presence a moment*
> *Which I want to draw in and forever to seize*
> *I truly appreciate how you've held your ear*
> *And listened to all of my future life fears.*
>
> *Vanessa*

Chapter 21

Vanessa, Charlotte

"My sister always said to me, shoot for the stars, for if you fail, you will always have the moon."

Vanessa

The year 1992 rolled around and in the fall, Charlotte and Vanessa started talking about where they wanted to go to college. The only thing Jeff and I were sure of was that it would be as far away from Phoenixville as they could get.

And it was. They chose California. Vanessa wanted to be near Darius, who was already enrolled at the University of California at Santa Cruz, and Charlotte just wanted to be in California period.

The general consensus from everyone we knew, including the doctors and parents at the hospital, was that we were crazy for letting them even think of going to school so far from home. But echoing in Jeff's and my minds was what had been our mantra throughout their lives: "Whatever you want to do in life, we will try to help in any way possible to make it happen."

So now, how could we tell them that what they wanted to do more than anything in the world wouldn't work because it was too far away from the security of our home, too far away from us, that we would miss them too much? How could we not let them follow their dreams when that was all they had? How could we tell them no, when all of their lives we had said, do all you can, and we will support you? In other words, how could we not let them go to live the lives they wanted to live? We couldn't. But oh it was hard.

Jeff and I always tried our best to give Charlotte and Vanessa a good life; they were our life. So how could we now stop supporting their dreams? The girls always thought of themselves as individuals first, the fact that they had cystic fibrosis second. We encouraged that notion and tried to raise them to be as independent as they could be in their situation.

We wanted what all parents want for their children, to see them soar in their own world, capturing as much happiness as possible, for as long as possible. We knew we would miss much in their lives because they would be so far away, and we did, but for us, it wasn't a choice. To see the excitement in their eyes, how ecstatic they were when they started putting together their plans, made the choice easier. We never could take that away from them.

Charlotte was accepted through early admission to Pepperdine University on a full scholarship to study art and writing. Vanessa was accepted at Mills College, a women's college near Berkeley, also on scholarship to study acting and writing.

When they received the news, they were on cloud nine; we were so proud of their determination and accomplishment, but we were also scared.

Chapter 22

Charlotte, Vanessa

"I got a break in the sense that if it wasn't for my parents, I wouldn't be here in California living the life I want to live. From day one, they have given me the life I wanted and have always supported it too. They didn't just say, 'I guess you can do that against our will.' They said, 'Yes, you can do that and we will help you.'"

Vanessa

"They let us come. They knew how happy we were out here."

Charlotte

So off to college they went, to start new lives filled with fierce determination, hope and promise, but also armed with packets of medicines, vitamins and uncertainty.

"When my mom was told we had CF, she decided that the best way she could help us was through nutrition. One of my mom's happiest days was when I swallowed an orange pit. Before I could swallow pills, my mom had to crush the vitamins and digestive enzymes and mix them into applesauce, which Charlotte and I had to eat before

each meal so we could digest our food. One day, I was eating an orange and I swallowed a pit. I ran and told my mom what I did and she said, "Wait, hold on," and brought out the Pancrease, our enzymes in capsules, to see if we could swallow one. We did and from then on we swallowed all our medicine and vitamins. It was a happy day for my mom."

"Now that we are at college, she sends us a month supply of aluminum foil packets, filled with our vitamins, enzymes, and some medicines. When we go into the hospital and bring the aluminum packets in Baggies, the minute the nurses see it they always ask, 'What is it, drugs?' So my mom is still very much involved in our everyday care, this is her way of feeling like she still has some control over the CF and one of the ways of keeping in touch, since we are no longer at home."

Vanessa

After a few weeks at college, we received the following letters from the girls, giving us a glimpse through their eyes of their lives growing up on the farm. I asked them if they had talked to one another about writing the letters. They said no, they didn't know the other had written one.

That is the phenomenon of twinhood, sometimes thinking the same thoughts at the same time. It happened quite a bit during their lifetime, but it still always amazed us.

Dear Mom and Dad,

There is so much I want to say, so maybe I'll start by saying what's never been said. My life is so different now and shall forever be altered. College is not why I'm so upset, it's a breeze; it's the bridge I've finally crossed over and the special stage in life left behind is my childhood. I've actually left you: the safety, love and precious memories behind are now a piece of my heart rather than reality. It will never be as before, Charlotte, Nanny, Dad, Mom and me together. I'm an adult now and ready to set out on my own separate path, alone.

Am I really here? How could my young life be truly over? It isn't though; we have our memories, which live inside us for eternity. Oh how the sacred memories dance now more than ever about my head. Wasn't it yesterday the daffodils bloomed in the spring, with daylong sledding with Charlotte as we were greeted with your smile, a wood burning stove and hot chocolate when we came inside? Bike rides with Nanny, Pop Pop, Charlotte, Mom and me to the cemetery. Forts, beeswax sculptures, painting, puppet shows, the smell of horse manure on dad, Harold's General Store, summer barbecues, truck rides on the cold red seat to school each morning, my elephant collection, the smells of Christmas, recitals at Lionville Elementary and Junior High, vacations to the islands. The smell of Dad's Aqua de Silva and your Chanel No. 5, you must be going out somewhere special, trips to the Bacons' house to hang out on the raft, Adirondacks, Arizona and the Florida Keys with Nanny, drives to Pat's house on the Outer Banks of North Carolina. Our trips each weekend to Aunt Gayle's house at the shore in the summer and sometimes winter for Kohrs custard, morning bike rides, Mac and Mancos pizza, miniature golf, and the beach with Missy.

Most of all I remember snuggling up in my footed PJ's (pink) with our chosen book and you reading to us in bed. Halloween, Easter, Thanksgiving, 4th of July, Christmas. These shall be forever changed, in good ways. I'm an independent woman now. No more trips to St. Christopher's for I now will have my own hospital—I've taken over my life. Your job as parents is over, but don't fret for you now have a better job, that of close friends. So now let go of me, for our paths now split and I spread my wings in freedom. It's time for me to accomplish the dreams molded and encouraged by my family. I will succeed and sharing my feats with you will be awesome, for we will hold on to the intimate memories of our lives together and cherish the future of friendship and love. Deep down I'll always be your little girl, yet entwined is the woman you've made me. Love the memories and cherish the future awaiting us, a future in which you'll witness the product of your love. You'll always be next to me in my heart.

    Your dearest friend
Love always,
Vanessa

P.S. Please take Teddy, he is the key to the past. He will always warm your heart as he did mine.

Vanessa was giving us our pink slip. We were being fired as parents. It made us smile.

Dear Mom and Dad,

  I was just sitting here thinking about how I never told you how much I love you both and think that you are the greatest parents. Sometimes my stubbornness just gets the better of me. The truth is I always knew that you both sacrificed everything for us and I love you more than I can express. I sit here and tell Christian and my friends how great the both of you are, yet I never told you how great, fabulous, and sweet you are. I have so many great memories that now override the bad. Remember picking vegetables from our garden, Pop Pop pushing us on our swing set, riding on daddy's tractor, playing board games, lobster nights, vacations, Grand Canyon, Dominican Republic, St. Thomas, Florida, Key West and the Star Lady, Disney World, Universal Studios Florida and California, years at the shore in Ocean City, Mack and Mancos pizza, morning bike rides and fresh orange juice, Kiawah, looking for sand dollars, Whale head, North Carolina, dolphins, and just small road trips, Crystal Cave, the zoo, elephants, Casa Maria's, picking out pumpkins on Halloween, hot apple cider, chopping down our own X-mas trees at Montgomery's, planting flowers, sledding, cross-country skiing, our horseback riding experiences. Tucson, Indian reservations, Amish country, Camp-hill milk (yuk), working out at the YMCA (yea right), Dad dancing to Jimmy Buffet 'Where do I go when the volcano blows,' the Wizard of Oz, Yeagers Hardware, Hallman's General Store, and so much more.

  It seems like yesterday when my sister and I were sporting braids, building forts in the woods, and catching toads and turtles in the springhouse. What about Playschool and Miss Marsha? Oh boy, I wonder if Miss Betty still has her jeep. I remember going to Betsy's before Neal was born and them saying they wanted little kids. I remember running around in sleepers, building cushion forts on the couch and drawing in crayon. It seems like yesterday when my sis and I would have the treat of going to Hallman's General Store and get gummy fishes. Those gummy fishes just don't taste as good anymore. I remember picking raspberries with nanny and pop. The smell, tastes, and feelings are so prominent now. I remember cuddling next to the fire after coming into the basement from the cold outside where my sister and I had made a snowman and igloos on our sledding hill. The blue flowers under the Japanese maple tree, and daffodils. I miss being able to lie in

96

the clover and find four leafers, I miss catching fire-flies and most of all I miss my good-night kisses, my hugs, and having not a care in the world. But most of all I miss you both.

It's weird to think it's all over, that I'm moving on with my life and nothing will ever be the same. I just want you to know how much I respect all that you have done for me, without it I would not be here today. I will always be here for you. If not in body, then in mind, because my love for you is unconditional. It is deeper than can be expressed. I may say things that hurt, but that is because I love you so much, weird is it not, but I am a weird cookie, ha ha. If ever you feel lonely just remember me as the little girl who clung to her mommy and daddy, because I'm still that little girl (just not as expressive). Remember and embrace all the little moments. The little girls who loved to perform and invent, because deep down I'm still that little girl who is clinging to her mommy and daddy.

I love you,
Charlotte

P.S. Tell nanny I love her and miss her.

Chapter 23

Vanessa, Charlotte

"As little girls, my sister and I loved to act. We performed in front of any audience that would indulge us. Our dream was to become actresses because they can touch so many with their words."

Vanessa

Vanessa's first semester at Mills College was an exciting, but trying time, her newly gained independence hard won. She loved her classes and was able to see Darius occasionally, but she didn't fit easily into campus life.

Like most students, she didn't like the food, and struggled daily to eat enough to maintain her weight, which was no easy task. Just walking to class became difficult, especially when she broke out in an itchy rash all over her body. It was determined she had an allergy to eucalyptus trees, which covered the entire campus, hence another medication added to her daily routine. In spite of it all, she did well in her classes, especially English and acting.

Two things occurred that first semester for which we are eternally grateful. First and foremost was the day she met her friend Stephanie.

Vanessa wasn't as outgoing as Charlotte and it took her longer to make friends. Thankfully, Stephanie appeared in her life soon after the semester began.

Her room was directly above Vanessa's and right from the start they hit it off, sharing stories and their passion for sweets. Stephanie once said it was as if Vanessa drew you in so intensely, you really didn't have a choice whether or not to be her friend; it was as if she willed it.

Their friendship lasted for the rest of Vanessa's life. Stephanie was always there to listen or brighten Vanessa's day at school, at home or in the hospital, bringing candy corresponding to the upcoming holiday, books, balloons and sometimes even a goldfish or two, fish bowl, food and all. We never knew what the surprise would be until she walked through the door, always with a big smile. She was a constant joy in Vanessa's life.

❧❦

Although the second occurrence pales in comparison, landing two roles in the school's most popular play of the year made Vanessa's semester. She had a full class schedule when she played the ghost of Christmas past and Scrooge's housekeeper in A Christmas Carol.

All she wrote to us about was the play. She relished spending all of her spare time at the theater and was in her glory when she learned The San Francisco Opera Company was creating a dress just for her as the ghost of Christmas past, layers of diaphanous silk that flowed around her as she glided across the stage.

On opening night, to make sure she would not cough during the performance, she took two Seldane tablets, a prescription antihistamine, instead of her usual one. The time came for her climactic scene, when the ghost of Christmas past has to cry. Now in every rehearsal she had no problem conjuring up the emotions she needed; she had many sad places to tap into. But that night, with two Seldane in her system, there was not a tear in sight, nor was there one drop of saliva in her mouth. Vanessa did a good job of faking it, but afterwards she still couldn't believe she could not cry on cue. She sailed through all the other performances, sticking to one Seldane, tears and saliva flowing freely.

But this was to be her last performance on stage. When she came home for Christmas break, she was exhausted and painfully thin. We noticed she was urinating a lot, but it didn't hit home until we went to the movies and every five minutes she was running to the bathroom.

Jeff said it could be a sign of diabetes so I called the doctor. When the blood glucose test came back over five hundred mg/dL, they couldn't believe she was still standing. She was hospitalized for a few weeks, but it took months at home for her to put on some weight, get her diabetes under control and gain some understanding of how this new disease would affect her cystic fibrosis.

Eating for Vanessa would never be the same again. The CF diet required ingesting as many calories as possible, with lots of fats, protein, and sugars. That was hard enough, but the diabetic diet was just the opposite so keeping her blood sugar under control became a constant struggle. She started out with oral medication, but it wasn't long before she had to have insulin shots every day, which increased in dosage and frequency as the disease progressed.

"It is a real drag having diabetes on top of the CF; it's a lose, lose situation because I need to eat a lot of foods for CF that are bad for diabetes, and yet to keep the diabetes under control you have to carefully watch what you eat, which doesn't help the CF. It took a long time and lots of problems before I got used to it and my solution is to take lots of insulin to cover the foods I want to eat."

Vanessa

She hated pricking her sore fingertips several times a day to test her blood so we tried other methods. We discovered her ear lobes worked the best so from then on, she walked around with bruised ears.

In some ways, developing diabetes made her angrier than having cystic fibrosis because she could see how it limited her life even more. And as a twin, she saw that Charlotte didn't have to worry about everything she put in her mouth or about passing out without warning, and it was hard to accept. Not that she ever wanted Charlotte to have diabetes, but being a twin is a very complicated relationship and theirs even more so because they were sick and relied so much on each other. This was more than accepting that she had diabetes, she also had to accept that Charlotte did not have to contend with all the problems associated with it, and as she would say, "It isn't fair."

Growing up, Vanessa always felt things came easier to Charlotte. If we scooped out ice cream for each of them, she felt Charlotte got more, which was funny because sometimes we purposely gave Vanessa more, but she didn't believe it.

It took time for her to adjust to this new threat in her life so instead of going back to Mills, she stayed home to gain some strength. She kept in constant touch with Darius and in the summer, he came out to see her and then wrote her this:

> "Vanessa, you are the sweetest person and your happiness means everything to me. It will work out, it always has. We just have to stick together and take it one step at a time. As long as you keep smiling, I will always be happy. Your smile brings joy to my world. I will love you forever."
>
> Darius

By the fall, feeling stronger and determined to begin again, Vanessa started at Loyola Marymount University near Los Angeles. Now closer to Darius, who had transferred to The University of California at San Diego and to Charlotte, with more support around her, she had a relatively good year. In one of her letters home she wrote:

> "I know Darius is the one I want to spend the rest of my life with. He truly loves me. It's nice having someone close who worries about me, and what I'm doing. He always makes sure I'm okay. It's rare finding someone so sensitive, but I guess we both lucked out, huh mom. Everything is starting to make sense again. I feel like I'm back on track towards my goal in life and this lies within acting and the love generated through Darius. We've become best friends and partners in life. He just fits."
>
> Vanessa

The following semester, while he was finishing his last year at UC, Darius and Vanessa moved in together. Vanessa loved their little apartment on the beach and spent her days taking a few classes at Loyola, writing and enjoying her life with Darius. They would never live apart again.

౿౿

While Vanessa was on the move, Charlotte spent three years at Pepperdine. She adjusted to college life quickly and thrived during the first year in the Malibu sunshine. Her room overlooked the Pacific Ocean and on one of my visits, we joked that I could move in and go back to school, a dream I must say was mostly mine.

In her sophomore year she joined a sorority, enrolled mostly in art and writing classes, and her love of watercolor deepened. When she was a teenager, I was taking watercolor classes at Rosemont College and she asked to try her hand at it. We were at the beach and she painted her Aunt Gayle's house. With no effort, she captured the essence of the place, while keeping her colors clean and vibrant. She was a natural and it became her favorite medium.

During her years at Pepperdine, Charlotte survived the Northridge earthquake, floods, mudslides, and a devastating season of fires in the canyons surrounding Malibu. She happened to be taking a nap during one of the disasters, when a rolling ball of fire roared down the canyon headed straight for the campus. All of the students had been evacuated into the gymnasium, but since she was sound asleep, she didn't hear the loudspeakers announcing the warning.

When she awoke and went outside, she thought she was in a war zone. Helicopters were flying overhead, dangling huge buckets of water under the body of the aircraft, with smoke everywhere. Someone from the helicopter saw her come out of the building and managed to get her to the safety of the gymnasium. A few weeks later, the floods and landslides came, but Charlotte continued on, not really afraid of the turmoil.

Her health was pretty good the first year. She always did more than she really could handle physically, but that was Charlotte. When she came home for Christmas break, she was tired and a little thin, but overall in much better shape than Vanessa. By summer break, she needed to go into the hospital for antibiotics and intensive respiratory therapy, but with lots of rest and good food, she gained weight, became stronger and was ready to go back to school in the fall.

Charlotte always tried to keep up a front with her friends and act as though her illness did not affect what she could accomplish, but after a while she couldn't do it all anymore. By the time her second and third year rolled around, it was taking a major toll on her health. She was hospitalized in Malibu several times for lung infections and for weeks had to walk to class with portable IV's in her pocket.

She napped frequently and tried to eat more to compensate for the weight loss from the now constant infections, even when it made her nauseous. Yet through all the struggles, she never let on how hard it was for her and she was determined to continue. When we asked, she always said she was happy and didn't want to change a thing. Meanwhile, we worried.

Charlotte met her best friend, Brooke, at Pepperdine and they decided to room together during Brooke's senior year. By this time, Charlotte was going to classes but was unable to participate in all the extra activities and Brooke was intent on finishing school. It was a good match for them at this time in their lives. On many weekends, they would stay in their pajamas, watch movies, eat and relax, something Charlotte required more and more. We will always be grateful to Brooke for caring so much about Charlotte and helping her through that year.

After Brooke graduated, she moved back to Denver, but still remained in Charlotte's life. When she married the following year at the Princeville Hotel on the island of Kauai, Charlotte was one of her bridesmaids and for five heavenly days, had the time of her life.

Chapter 24

Charlotte, Vanessa

"As we went off to college to follow our acting dreams, our family lovingly supported us with encouragement that we would make our mark on the world. We had hoped that we could impact the world through acting, however, due to our failing health, this would not be possible. With the realization that acting was not an option anymore, we found renewed hope through our writing and painting.

"As children, books and flights into our imagination were our escape. When we were twelve, we wrote "Danny's Dream." So we used that experience to write and help others escape into that world. We have always been able to write, no matter how sick we were.

"My parents read to us all the time. Imagination was our play tool. It helps people and kids who are sick. They can read or look at a book and their imagination can go anywhere, even though they can't leave the house. I know how that is. Even though I can't be on stage now, I can express myself through writing.

"At this point, Charlotte and I realize we can still impact the world through our words and paintings by telling our story about living with cystic fibrosis. We have completed five books and enjoy sharing them with friends and family and now we would love to touch many more lives by having them published. It gives us something to live for. So *the actress I wished to be, turned into the writer I am today and always was within me."*

Vanessa

"When I wrote 65 Roses, I was really sick that day in the hospital and had just gotten up from a nap. The story is about a tree and a flower and what it is like to have cystic fibrosis. It just made so much sense when I wrote it and it all came to me in that one day. It was great to get it out and know that the story will live longer than I will; that people will look at this book when I am not here and see my paintings. It meant a lot to me to write it. I felt like I got it off my chest."

Charlotte

*I*t became apparent to Charlotte and Vanessa, to all of us, that they no longer had the stamina for acting. Writing and illustrating books allowed them to utilize the creative energy they always had in life and gave them hope that they could still make a mark in this world.

Chapter 25

Caleb, Charlotte

"We took a roller coaster ride the weekend we met and never looked back."

Charlotte

In the fall of her junior year, Charlotte met the love of her life. She was visiting Vanessa and Darius in San Diego, when Caleb, a childhood friend of Darius', arrived with his mom, Carol, and his sister, Bre, to look at colleges. When Charlotte and Caleb were introduced, it was love at first sight.

That weekend, they went to the movies and afterward rode the roller coaster at the beach and as Vanessa has said, "The rest is history."

The night before driving back home, he asked his mom if a friend could ride up with them to Pepperdine, since his sister wanted to see the school anyway. The following morning, when Carol and Bre drove up to Vanessa's apartment to pick up Caleb and his "friend", they were astonished to see Charlotte and Caleb sitting on a bench wrapped together in a blanket. Here they were expecting a guy, not a girl, and certainly not two people obviously infatuated with one another.

On the drive up the coast, in true Charlotte spirit, she talked the whole way. Not long into the conversation, she started coughing. "Don't worry, I'm not contagious. I just have cystic fibrosis so I cough a lot, but you can't catch it." And that was all she said about it.

"Oh!" was all Carol said on the subject, but a few years later she told me she was stunned when Charlotte made the statement so nonchalantly.

At the time, Carol didn't know exactly what cystic fibrosis was, but she knew it was not good. When she arrived home and looked it up in the medical encyclopedia, her fears were confirmed, but they never influenced how she already felt about Charlotte. She told me later that from the first time they met, she immediately fell under her charm.

A week later, Caleb flew down to Malibu from Marin County where he was working, to celebrate Charlotte's twenty-first birthday. They went out with several friends to Gladstone's where they feasted on Charlotte's favorite food, lobster.

After that weekend, Caleb and Charlotte saw one another as much as possible. Over the next six months, Caleb often made the six-hour trip down Interstate 5, onto Route 101 then straight to the Malibu coast. Sometimes Charlotte followed the same roads, only north, in "Freddie", her navy blue Saab. One thing we all knew, they were indelibly connected. Charlotte always said that Caleb was her angel here on earth and it turned out to be true.

A few weeks before the end of spring semester, Charlotte became sick and quickly lost a great deal of weight fighting the constant infection in her lungs. She decided to fly home early without completing her last week of classes. Although she was extremely disappointed that she wasn't able to complete the semester, she really didn't have a choice; this time her body would have its way.

Charlotte spent the summer first in the hospital and then on home care, conscientiously doing all of her meds and treatments and working hard to gain back some of the weight she had lost. When she started feeling stronger, we found out why she was so determined. Her goal was to move back out to California to live with Caleb.

While she was home working on gaining her strength back, Caleb searched for an apartment, which was no easy task in Marin County, with its many expensive houses. After many disappointments, he found the perfect apartment in Larkspur, a complex high on a hill with a view, an elevator and walking distance to his work. Caleb thought of it all, even down to the cozy furnishings. By late July, the apartment was ready, so Charlotte could fly out and they could start their new life together.

⌀⌀

Meanwhile, Darius had graduated from UC San Diego in May, and decided to move back to the San Francisco area where his family lived. He and Vanessa found a cute apartment in Mill Valley, only fifteen minutes from Charlotte and Caleb, and in the opposite direction, fifteen minutes to my sister's home. With their furniture, some antiques from my sister, artwork from Darius's dad, and all of Vanessa's little treasures, they created a lovely place to live.

After they moved in, Darius began working in San Francisco, while Vanessa spent her time writing, working on her children's book and keeping up with all of her daily treatments.

She even raised a litter of kittens, although when the feral cat first appeared on their deck, they mistakenly thought that "she" was a "he". After feeding the cat for a while, Vanessa noticed a change in its weight and mentioned this to me on the phone a few times, "Mom, Sebastian is getting really fat." I had my suspicions about why and soon they were confirmed. Yes, she was pregnant.

So her name was changed to Sebastiani. Being a feral cat, she never really lived in the house, but would come in to take care of her kittens. Vanessa was told if the feral kittens were found outside by the animal control agency, they would have been destroyed and that was why they were living in the house.

Soon Vanessa was immersed in the pleasure of mothering four kittens. Every morning she would wake up to four little tongues licking her and meowing. Like twins, they paired off together and each pair was distinctly different; one wild and crazy, aptly named Thelma and Louise, the other quiet and sedate, hence Franklin and Eleanor. They gave her a fun reason to get out of bed.

When it was time to find them homes, she insisted they go as pairs; she felt they belonged together, just like twins. Darius' dad and his wife, Katie, took Thelma and Louise, and Franklin and Eleanor went to a retired couple with no children. Vanessa was thrilled she still would be able to visit them and watch them grow.

✂⊗

This was a good time in all of our lives. It was comforting to see the girls settled with men they loved, and at work on their books. They spoke constantly on the phone about ideas and changes. And although their illness was always present through all the treatments they had to do each day, they also had lives they were happy with. That was the most important thing.

✂⊗

Jeff and I have always thought that the girls lived longer because they were loved and in love with Caleb and Darius. There was such a bond between them and the two young men; it made them want to stay in this world and fight to live for as long as they did. We are so grateful for all we shared with Caleb and Darius and even though in the end there was such sorrow, it was delicately wrapped in many moments of joy and laughter, bringing such richness to all of our lives.

Choosing to love someone, even though that person has a terminal illness, is a gift, not only to the person who is ill, but also to the person who makes the choice to love. And it is a choice. For Darius and Caleb, I don't think it ever was a conscious one. They fell in love with the girls and decided to share their lives with them, no matter what the future held. But for their families, it must have been difficult to know that the women their sons loved would die young, and that their sons would face overwhelming sadness ahead. But throughout all the years, although I am sure the doubt was there, they never expressed any doubts to us and they loved the girls through it all. We will always be grateful.

Chapter 26

Vanessa, Charlotte

"They always took the time to be with us and used all the money they had and focused it all on us. Their lives were our lives, it was very special, it still is special, they may live in PA, but they are still as close as home."

Charlotte

Soon, the girls' being so far away from home meant more than our not talking face to face, sharing their everyday lives, or hugging and kissing them good night. It meant we were not there when they were in crisis.

The first time we had an emergency call from three thousand miles away, I was working at The Children's Hospital of Philadelphia. At 1:30 in the afternoon, I received a call from Charlotte's doctor at the medical center in San Francisco. "Charlotte is in respiratory distress. I don't think she will be alive by the time you can get a flight out here."

"Tell her we are coming," was all I could say.

As I frantically called Jeff, a colleague managed to get us on the 5:06, the last direct flight out of Philadelphia to San Francisco. This would become a flight I would know all too well in the coming years.

I ran and grabbed a cab to my house, where Jeff was waiting. When we arrived at the airport, we called the hospital in San Francisco before just barely making our flight. We were told Charlotte was holding on and those few words were what we held on to as we sat silently hand in hand, too stunned to speak during the long flight.

When we landed, we ran through San Francisco airport to the exit where my sister was waiting. We jumped in her car, afraid to ask. She broke the silence. "Charlotte has responded to the medications and is actually doing much better." Later, my sister said she never saw anyone so scared and disoriented as we were when we rushed through the airport doors. If she only knew what was going on inside us; that was even more frightening.

When we hurried into Charlotte's room, she was sitting up in bed looking much better than we expected, with a big smile on her face as we ran to her side. The doctor said he realized after he called that she had a severe constriction in her airways, similar to an asthma attack, which opened up after a large dose of the steroid Prednisone was administered through an IV.

I didn't bring up the fact that days earlier on the phone I had suggested that he increase her steroid dose, but at the time he didn't agree. I also asked him that day to call her physicians back east to discuss her particular problems and had them standing by to speak to him, but to no avail. He didn't call.

I understood that Charlotte was a fairly new patient and that he was not familiar with all the subtleties of her body, but not listening to a patient or to her mom, both of whom knew her body better than anyone else, remained a bone of contention during her time at this medical center. Why wouldn't a physician want to have all the information about a patient in a disease so complex? It didn't make sense and we found it more and more difficult in a large hospital to be heard through all the layers of hierarchy.

Little did we know that this would be the beginning of many frantic trips to California, never knowing when the plane touched down, if we would have the time to say goodbye.

Chapter 27

Caleb, Charlotte

"When I met Charlotte, I don't think it was my choice to love her or not to love her, to leave her or to stay. I knew this person made me the happiest I've ever been so that was the direction I went."

Caleb

On December 25, 1997, Caleb asked Charlotte to marry him. In a documentary filmed a year and a half later, Caleb and Charlotte discussed getting married:

Caleb: "We chose to marry because if we are going to have a shorter time together we need to do the things that make us happy, things that we can celebrate with all of our friends and family—while she can enjoy it—while we both can enjoy it, so we decided we wanted to be married."

Charlotte: "I wanted to get married while I was still healthy enough to walk down the aisle, although it did go through my mind that it's not fair to marry him because it was kind of like dooming him to being sad eventually, but we are so close and we can't deny that. It's such a hard lesson to learn at a young age, but I believe that people who have good relationships, when their partner dies, they are able to go on and find someone else, and continue to have a good life because they don't feel their partner would be mad at them because they shared so much together. As long as we can be together now, it will be okay."

Caleb, smiling: "She couldn't stop me anyway. We want to spend as much time together as possible and we want to do as many things as we can. I've considered every aspect of our lives from where I work to where we take vacations to what we do on the weekends and after work to be together as much as possible. We love each other so we are going to be married; it's the next step. So who cares about her illness, that's a bump, a huge bump, but it's just a bump."

Charlotte: "It is something we deal with everyday, but when you find someone that you're this close to, nothing else matters. Some people go their entire lives and find no one that they have such a bond with; we were lucky. No matter what happens, it's worth it. I love Caleb more than anything in the world and he wanted to marry me so...and then laughing 'I don't know why.'"

৶৻

It had been only a year since they met and Charlotte had never been happier. We were thrilled and gave them a diamond, which a local artist in Mill Valley designed a ring around.

A garden wedding was planned for the following August in Pennsylvania at the country home of our long time friends, Pat and Ray Jones. Preparations began long distance until Charlotte decided to come home in early summer to gain some strength and get ready for the big event.

Flying had become more difficult for the girls now and when they flew, they required oxygen. When Charlotte slowly walked off the plane, she was extremely thin and weak. After a few days at home, she agreed to be admitted to Paoli Memorial Hospital, where I was working, to start on her routine intravenous antibiotics and increased respiratory treatments.

A week went by and she showed no signs of improvement. We brought her home on home care with a low-grade temperature. As the day progressed, her breathing became more and more labored and at times she was gasping for air. It was scary for her, which made her breathe even faster, compounding the problem.

We finally called the paramedics and she was taken by ambulance to a local hospital, struggling to breathe even with the oxygen on high, the mask pressed tightly to her face. There was little the local hospital could do and we finally convinced her to go to St. Christopher's Hospital for Children, the hospital she used before she went away to college. She didn't want to go when she returned home because it was over an hour away and she was now over nineteen years old, the cut-off age for patients.

I called their doctors at the hospital and they agreed to waive the rule because she would not be continuing there after she married. She would be moving back to California.

After being admitted, she underwent all the routine tests and was scheduled to start on another round of four intravenous antibiotics for the rampant lung infection, some new respiratory medicines and increased therapy. But when they tried to insert the PIC line for her intravenous antibiotics, the vein was blocked. The x-ray showed there was too much scar tissue for the tube to be threaded into the vein. The only other alternative was a port, which Charlotte did not want before her wedding day because it would be hard to find a dress to cover it. It also meant that she was getting sicker.

Because Charlotte was reluctant to get the port, another physician we had never met before explained a new procedure being used. Dye would be injected into the vein, and the doctor would follow the path on a monitor to try to thread the PIC line up the vein in the arm. He said he was confident this would work.

Since we needed to get the antibiotics started as soon as possible, and with very few options left, Charlotte agreed to the procedure and was taken in to surgery. I watched from an adjoining room through a large window with the IV nurse.

I stopped watching after the first try, only glancing up for brief moments. The IV nurse turned away after the second try, but the physician continued, determined to make this work. Charlotte lay flat on her back staring at the ceiling, her eyes full of tears that rolled silently down her face, as she tried not to show the pain and disappointment, with each failed try.

When it was all over, the pure white sheet underneath her was soaked in blood. All this and it didn't work. The doctor suggested they try again the next day on the other arm and in unison we said absolutely not. She was never going through that again.

Charlotte agreed to the port in her chest, her only choice if she wanted to live. It was placed in an artery near her collarbone in her right upper chest, a bump the size of a walnut shell, the size of a grapefruit in her eyes.

The wedding dress she eventually chose covered the port entirely. Afterwards she said the port made her life easier since she was on antibiotics so frequently that the port access made the treatment less stressful.

A few days into her hospital stay, the doctors recommended sinus surgery to help clear out some of the infection and polyps in her nasal passages, which they thought could be making her lung infections worse. So, surgery was scheduled.

She also was dangerously thin and needed to begin tube feeding at night for extra nutrition. Cystic fibrosis patients generally need to eat at least twice as many calories a day as a person their same size, just to keep their weight relatively stable. It takes a great deal of calories to fight the constant lung infection and Charlotte was not able to eat enough to even come close to her sustainable weight.

The tube feeding required Charlotte to thread a long thin tube up her nose, down her throat and into her stomach, carefully avoiding placing it into her lung. It was a nasty thing to have to do every night.

I would sit with her and apply the sterile petroleum jelly to the end of the new tube. She then would take the tube in her hand and with a faraway look, stare at it for a while before threading it slowly into her nose. Sometimes she would begin to gag and had to pull it out because it had started into the passageway of her lungs, only having to do the whole process all over again. When it was finally threaded all the way in, we still had to make sure it was in her stomach and not her lungs, even though she most likely would have known it was in the wrong place. We had to take a syringe and inject air into the nasal tube, listening for the sound of bubbles through a stethoscope placed on her tummy.

When the nasal tube was in place, we shook the five cans of high calorie supplement, totaling two thousand five hundred calories, popped open the cans and instantly the smell of cake batter filled the room. Sounds yummy, but trust me, it isn't. We poured all the cans into a plastic IV bag and hung it on the pole. Then we unclamped the lock on the tube and watched the cream-colored liquid flow down to the end pushing out any air pockets that could be released into her stomach, which can cause discomfort.

It created a sticky mess if you didn't get it clamped off in time which meant it would flow out the end of the tube. It had the consistency of glue from the high fat and sugar content and was difficult to clean up, leaving a sickening sweet smell that would linger no matter what you did.

Then, we would thread the tube through the monitor, set the time and flow for the night, usually eight hours, then attach it to the other end already placed into her stomach, and finally, we were ready to turn on the power.

The rhythmic clicking of the machine filled the nighttime silence and many times during the night, if the tube clogged or if the machine was just being sensitive, which happened frequently, a piercing alarm would go off.

Before starting all of this, Charlotte would already have finished her hour-and-a-half-long respiratory treatments earlier in the evening because the coughing would make her throw up the tube and that would mean she would have to start all over again.

Finally, with five enzymes and numerous vitamins in one hand and a big glass of water in the other, Charlotte would pop the whole lot in her mouth and in one gulp wash them down. Her nightly routine was done. It was now time to put her head on the pillow and try to sleep.

⁂

She came home from the hospital two weeks after the nasal surgery to recover, weighing only ninety pounds and that was after gaining back some weight. For the rest of the summer, she was diligent about her nighttime feedings; her goal was to be healthy for her wedding day.

The nasal tube feeding she endured every night squelched what little appetite she had left, but perseverance paid off and soon she began gaining some weight and strength. Besides the nighttime feeding, she required four respiratory treatments a day, three consecutive doses of intravenous antibiotics lasting two and a half hours every six hours.

She was on oxygen all night and most of the day, her fifty foot oxygen cord snaking throughout the house, following her wherever she went. On top of this, we had lots to do for the wedding and were always busy. The summer flew by.

Chapter 28

Charlotte, Caleb

"Caleb, you've made my life complete. You've made all my dreams come true, which sounds so hokey, but it's the truth. Everyday is important and we live everyday to the fullest. You just are incredible. You make me want to live. I wouldn't be here without you."

Charlotte

When Charlotte said she wanted to release butterflies at her wedding I didn't try to dissuade her. Okay, maybe a little. I knew this would mean more work and I was feeling overwhelmed as it was. But, as usual, we found a way.

We ordered the butterflies three months in advance. Three weeks before the wedding, the overnight box came in the mail containing one hundred and twenty chrysalises, one hundred and twenty small white pyramid-shaped boxes and a set of instructions. The next morning, Charlotte and I constructed all of the boxes, then carefully placed one chrysalis in each box and secured the tops.

We now had one hundred and twenty little triangular homes in which, hopefully, these chrysalises would magically transform into butterflies. According to the instructions, the butterflies would emerge within three weeks. They could survive only about five days in the box before they had to be released to find food. So timing and temperature were vital.

Temperature was the most difficult to control. It was the end of July and we were in a typical Philadelphia heat wave with high humidity. Our window air conditioners were on full blast because Charlotte needed the humidity low and the temperature cool.

The butterflies required a steady temperature of seventy-six to seventy-eight degrees with no fluctuations or drafts. After trying several locations, I found a spot near the air conditioner, with no draft and not too hot or cold, and we waited.

After three weeks, as the directions stated, we checked to see if the butterflies had emerged. I thought I could hear a rustle of wings when I picked up the first box, but I wasn't certain. A visual check of a few boxes was also recommended.

I carefully opened one just a crack and a butterfly flew out. I guess I didn't learn my lesson and wanted to make sure they had all hatched, so I checked another and that too escaped. With Charlotte's help, after chasing them through the house, I was finally able to get them back into their boxes.

And this was no easy feat. The box was triangular so we had to simultaneously hold all three sides almost closed while trying to get the butterfly back in without damaging its wings or its fragile body. After several tries, we manage to get the two back in their respective boxes, but we were sure we had exhausted their store of energy to survive the next five days. So we now figured we were down to one hundred and eighteen, if we were lucky.

Amidst all the wedding details that still needed to be attended to, the everyday care of Charlotte and Vanessa, who arrived home at the beginning of August to be a part of all the plans, was my first priority.

Vanessa came home very thin, but did not seem to need a hospital stay. Her diabetes was a problem, so we tried to work on that while attending to all of the other things we were trying to accomplish in a short period of time.

It was hectic trying to keep everything straight. I had to have oxygen delivered to our home, to Pat's home for the wedding and also to the hotel where Charlotte and Caleb would be spending their wedding night. Since Charlotte was still on home care, I had to make sure she had all of her medicines and IV's delivered to the house. On top of that I had to deal with the caterer, flowers, and all the last minute details, and we had many people flying in from California.

⚜

August 16, 1998 was one of the happiest days of Charlotte's life. With friends, family and lots of lobster and champagne, she married the love of her life, Caleb, and together their lives were complete.

The day was magical, glorious, and absolutely exhausting. Charlotte needed frequent rests as her friend Brooke and Vanessa helped her dress. Brooke took over applying her makeup, as Charlotte constantly sipped cold water and tried to keep the oxygen tube snaking down from her nose out of the way. When she was ready, she looked utterly beautiful in her long ivory dress and veil. She glowed. Oh, the magic of happiness.

Meanwhile, the afternoon temperatures were rising and the humidity was building as the photographer tried to take as many pictures as possible before the start of the ceremony. It drained Charlotte even before the ceremony began; beads of sweat were forming at the edge of her hairline, darkening the corners of her upswept hair. We had to take off her stockings and the crinoline slip under her dress to cool her down. Between each take, she grabbed for her oxygen, but looking back at the pictures, one would never think she was struggling.

All I kept thinking was, "How is she going to do this?" but that was not a question I needed to ask. Charlotte always rose to the occasion. She could be struggling to breathe or in pain, yet she could always manage that smile to make you feel better, to make you feel that she was okay, sometimes revealing more than she thought to those who knew her so well. I still think how important it was for her to make everyone around her feel good and how successful she was in her efforts.

⚜

When Charlotte was ready, she took one final deep breath, removed her oxygen, and with Vanessa by her side, radiantly descended the circular staircase. She waited arm in arm with her dad at the wrought iron entrance gate to the walled garden. When the harpist began to play, they slowly walked down the aisle, past friends and family, to Caleb waiting at the fountain. Her dad lifted Charlotte's veil, kissed her and placed her hand into Caleb's.

The ceremony included several readings from friends and the vows they had written for one another. After the official ceremony was over, Vanessa announced she wanted to read a poem she had written for Charlotte and Caleb. Everyone laughed because it was so Vanessa. Charlotte had the spotlight all day and now it was Vanessa's turn for a few minutes. It was just the way it was, and she began the poem with the names they called one other when they were young and couldn't pronounce their real names:

> As Dee Dee and Daw Dee we were born,
> Mates from birth and never torn,
> And although as people we weren't the same,
> We fought through our differences and friends we became.
> She was the optimist, friends always first,
> I am the stubborn one with perfectionist thirst.
> We could always count on Charlotte's big smile,
> Where I am the one who smirks with style.
> Charlotte accepted and I pursue,
> But who ever knew,
> That our taste in men would be one and the same,
> And she ended up marrying Darius' best friend by name.
> It must have been fate that linked them as two,
> Two timely visits to San Diego on cue.
> What was made in Heaven, met on earth,
> To Caleb and Charlotte, to joy and mirth
> May happiness surround you with lucks' sweet chords
> And strength sustain you with steadfast swords
> And if tears of sadness begin to fall
> The love you share will conquer all
> For you are never alone from this day forth
> You are his south and he is your north
> So if you are misdirected and cannot find your way
> Look towards each other and it will be okay
> And with these boxes let us unleash your wings
> To represent the new life forged by your rings

For if you walk as one and evolve together
Your hearts will be strong
And last forever.

When Vanessa had finished, she kissed Charlotte and Caleb and everyone released the butterflies from the boxes placed on their chairs. They filled the air, hovering all around us, their orange and black wings furiously fluttering before they greedily landed on the surrounding flowers, tasting the sweetness and savoring their well-won freedom. Some flew away, but many stayed to keep us company.

Eventually, the guests began wandering off to see the rest of the property and gather for the reception. Pat had said she wanted to show us something special, so Caleb, Charlotte, Jeff and I followed her to the far garden wall where an espalier pear tree was growing, its flat branches spread out in long, straight rows, donning all its summer leaves.

She pointed to a cluster of dense leaves. When we moved in to get a closer look, we saw two pears, side-by-side. She said it was a special surprise because the tree had never produced fruit before and now there were only two pieces of fruit, right next to each other, in honor of Charlotte and Caleb.

છ૭

There was candlelight dining and dancing throughout the evening. When the reception was winding down, Charlotte and Caleb escaped to a small hotel nearby. It had been a very long day, actually a very long summer for her. At five in the morning, we received a call from Caleb. "Charlotte had a very bad night. Can you pick us up? She needs to come home." Jeff drove over as Caleb carried her down the stairs. Soon, she was tucked into her own bed and slept soundly between her IV treatments and therapies.

What we were learning oh too well was that weddings or special times do not fit easily into a chronically ill person's life. Illness, unfortunately, can never be left behind for a minute; it is there every second of the day, every moment in the night, influencing every detail of how you plan, how you live. Charlotte hated this aspect of her disease. She loved the spontaneity of life and here she was, twenty-three years old, and it just wasn't feasible anymore.

123

Chapter 29

Caleb, Charlotte

"I always tried to look at each of them as a person, not as their illness. I tried to think what would I want for them if it was me, and I wanted them to live as normal a life as possible, with hopes and dreams and not define themselves as a sick person first. Jeff and I always said to them that you can do whatever you want to do, and they did. It enables us to live with what is happening now because we feel we have done everything we could. Not having a big house or car really didn't matter because we had time. I look at the girls and I think how rich they have made our lives. Money could never make up for that. It has been a wonderful life because they are so positive and brave."

Pat

A week passed and we all decided it would be best if Caleb flew back to California without Charlotte. She needed to be home for a few more weeks to regain her strength and finish her course of treatment. She wanted to be as healthy as possible for their dream-come-true honeymoon, twelve days at the Four Seasons Hotel on the island of Maui in Hawaii, a wedding gift from her Aunt Jan and Uncle Ross. Charlotte was so excited; she could hardly wait.

I needed the time to coordinate all the oxygen, medicines and supplements she would need in California and Hawaii, while she needed time to rest before the trip.

∅⌀

Meanwhile, after the wedding, Vanessa and Darius flew back to California, even though Vanessa was tired and not as well as I would have liked her to be. A few weeks later, Charlotte flew back to California for a week before starting her honeymoon.

Several days after Charlotte and Caleb arrived in Hawaii, Vanessa was admitted to the medical center in San Francisco. She was very thin, her diabetes was out of control and she was having trouble breathing. We did not know at the time that this stay would last over two months.

Like Charlotte, she now needed a port for antibiotics because her veins were no longer viable for a PIC line. Vanessa decided she did not want the port in her chest, she wanted it in her lower arm, which posed more problems than the chest, but she got her way and the surgery was performed so she could start her antibiotic therapy.

After a few weeks in bed at the hospital, Vanessa was encouraged to get some needed exercise. Attached to her IV pole by dangling tubes of medicine, she shuffled round and round the hallway on the twelfth floor. In her travels, she met a woman named Lois who was sitting in her doorway. Lois had recently learned that her colon cancer had spread and there was nothing more they could do. She was overwhelmed by the news.

Vanessa began visiting Lois every day and they became fast friends. In one of Lois' daughter's daily phone calls, Lois said to her, "It's okay that you aren't able to come, Vanessa's here and I'm reading the books she and her sister wrote."

∅⌀

Meanwhile, Charlotte and Caleb were enjoying their honeymoon in Hawaii, even though they barely left the grounds of the Four Seasons Hotel. They liked relaxing by the pool reading and enjoying the warmth of the sun.

Charlotte decided not to do her tube feeding, even though it had all been sent beforehand and was waiting in her room; it was her

126

honeymoon and she wanted some respite from reality. Instead, she tried to eat more, but by now, especially with no appetite, it could never be enough. The bacteria in her lungs were greedy, voraciously gobbling up calories twenty-four hours a day, seven days a week with no relief. No amount of food could satisfy them anymore.

By the end of their honeymoon, Charlotte was very weak. Touching down at San Francisco airport, she went straight from paradise to reality, the hospital. In twelve days, all the weight she had struggled so hard over the summer to gain was lost. Her reluctance and sadness were evident when we talked about tube feeding. "I just can't face putting that tube down my nose every night anymore and I know I will die if I don't do something." A permanent stomach tube was the next step in the constant battle against this disease. She silently accepted.

"Now that I always have an infection in my lungs and I am always sick, I just never have an appetite, which stinks for me because I always LOVED food. I was always one of those people who could sit down and eat two cheese steaks and French fries. I would just say "Come on, bring it on, and Caleb would always say, 'How come you are so little?' I loved food, I just loved it, it was one of my favorite pastimes, eating, and now one of the hardest things for me is I cannot eat; it makes me sick to my stomach. It was such a love and now it's been taken away. My husband can't stand it. He constantly says 'Come on Charlotte, you can do it.' So actually the stomach tube has made it much easier on our relationship because he is not always saying 'Come on Charlotte, you've got to eat, come on you have to eat that last pea.' The life of a CF patient is you are always being force fed."

❧❧

Vanessa was still in the hospital and Charlotte was now just down the hall. After a few days, when Charlotte was up to it, she met Lois. Late that evening, Lois's daughters Patty and Melinda arrived at the hospital to visit their mom. Vanessa and Charlotte were still in Lois' room talking with her and a few other patients. Lois said to her daughters after everyone had left the room, "Wherever Charlotte and Vanessa are, it seems others congregate."

Patty said that after her mom met Vanessa her whole outlook changed. "It was a bad time for our family, and it was worse because my sister and I couldn't be at the hospital as much as we wanted. I felt guilty for not being with my mom, but once she met Vanessa, her outlook improved so much. She connected with Vanessa and Charlotte right away. She loved them right off the bat. Part of the reason for my mother's mental and emotional improvement, is that Vanessa and Charlotte had such an open, honest way of dealing with their terminal illness. They talked to my mother about dying. She was so afraid and then suddenly she wasn't afraid anymore. It was such a lonely feeling, but they reached out to my mom. They talked about the afterlife and gave her comfort. They were both wise beyond their years."

Lois went home a few weeks later and sold her house in Sausalito. She decided to rent a house high on a hill in Tiburon, overlooking San Francisco Bay, something she had always wanted to do. During the last six months of her life, she surrounded herself with the breathtaking views of the harbor she loved.

During this time, Charlotte and Vanessa had a chance to meet Lois's family and they visited them several times in her new home. The day before Lois died, Patty called to let them know she was dying and they went over.

During the evening, Lois asked Vanessa and Charlotte to come into her bedroom to say good-bye. When they left her room, each was carrying an antique quilt she had given them "to keep them warm at night." The quilts remained on the girls' beds until the day they died. They now are on my bed.

Vanessa wrote the following poem for Lois, which Patty read at her memorial service. The angel pin the girls gave to their mom months before, was buried with her:

"Lois"

Two months ago I was alone
Except for a nurse and hospital phone
I sat in the darkness, lit up by TV
Harassed by the interns and a beeping IV
But my nights soon changed, they were filled with a light
With a woman named Lois and a mutual fight
The stories she told captured my ear
A life of adventure and lived without fear
She helped me see the beauty she'd hold

To listen and laugh and erase my cold
And for those few moments a fog was burned
With our mutual plight, my life then turned
I learned to embrace the life I've been dealt,
Love now engrosses the anger I felt.
Thank you for helping me see the light ahead
Not regretting the past and hatred instead.
And when we cross over, we'll embrace the love,
We stitched over time to fit like a glove.
And those we chose to include in our lives,
Will help spawn our memories and it's there we'll survive.
So if a soft breeze kisses your cheek,
Don't be sad, don't be meek,
For it's Lois's way to say hello,
To her loved ones, down here below.
She simply moved on to a special place,
Where she can live and her pain be erased.
And from here she wants her loved ones to know,
To prosper forth, to live, to grow.
And from her place she'll watch them with love,
And blanket our earth with joy from above.
With sun she will warm us, and rain she will weep,
And bring us darkness so we can sleep.
And if we miss her and shed a tear,
She will find a way to remind us she is near.
By a soft spring shower, or a bird's sweet song,
She will always be there to help us along.
And until our time comes to meet her above,
She will live in our memories and thrive in our love.

Patty remained in the girls' lives until they died and now she remains in mine.

Chapter 30

Darius, Vanessa

"That is why I have been afraid to get in touch with my friends recently because I am so different than I was just a year ago. I'm afraid to tell them 'Well look, I'm sick, I'm dying, I'm not like I was.' And then they get sad and it's hard to see that they're sad. I don't want to see them sad. It's still me. I'm still here, hey, I'm still breathing so...

"Darius has seen me at my healthiest times and he has seen me at my worst times and he is still there and loving me for who I am, tummy tube and all, Prednisone puff and all. He finds me beautiful no matter how I look. In the hospital with fifty tubes sticking out of me, 'I think you're beautiful, you're my boo.' He calls me boo! Well okay, it's all that counts."

Vanessa

C harlotte went home from the hospital after two weeks with her new stomach tube for nightly feedings and dependent on oxygen twenty-four hours a day. Vanessa remained behind.

Vanessa's body was not responding to the mix of four antibiotics flowing through her veins, and her diabetes was still out of control. She was getting thinner by the day trying to fight the raging infection in her lungs, frustrated and confused with what she could eat to satisfy both diseases and gain weight. She was five foot six and weighed eighty-five pounds.

During this hospital stay, Vanessa and I struggled in our battle to be heard through so many layers of staff at this large teaching hospital. It took forever to get anything done. When she needed her insulin increased, we would wait hours and hours, sometimes all day, for the orders to be approved, charted and the medicine ordered. All the while Vanessa was trying to remain coherent and not lapse into a coma. Nothing seemed to speed up the process.

Most of the interns, residents and staff taking care of Vanessa welcomed her input. Who knew her body better than Vanessa, and she could and would articulate the many problems and issues surrounding her care. But in reality, at a large teaching hospital only the head of the department makes the ultimate decisions and it was extremely frustrating because he was not part of these discussions and didn't see the subtle everyday changes in her condition.

By now, Vanessa was not able to eat or hold anything down. She was dangerously thin and growing weaker by the hour. She had even lost the strength to cough. I had been arguing back and forth for five days saying they should start hyper alimentation, the same procedure she had at birth to nourish her while waiting for her body to pass the blockage. Only this time she needed the nutrients to fight the raging lung infection, complicated by the need for increased steroids to open up her airways.

We all knew there were risks with both treatments, but at this point it was the only option, since her blood gas numbers were falling and her carbon dioxide level was rising rapidly. Finally, on Friday morning, after waiting all week, with all the staff in agreement, the treatments were ordered, but at the end of the day, the head of the department cancelled them before going home for the weekend because of complications associated with the treatment.

The resident came by to tell me everything was cancelled once again, even though he agreed it was urgent and should have been started, but the department head did not think it merited the risks. I wanted to scream. Vanessa was too weak to respond.

That night, with two forms of oxygen going, and only two nurses covering the entire floor, Vanessa and I struggled all through the night to keep her conscious. I pressed the call button over and over, but no one responded. I knew that because of the excess oxygen her carbon dioxide level was climbing, and by five in the morning, I was screaming for a nurse, as I sat on Vanessa's bed, holding the mask to her face, trying to keep her oxygen level stable. Vanessa was drifting into a coma so I jumped up and yelled out the door in the direction of the nurse's station for someone to help me. Afraid I would lose her, I didn't want to leave the room.

Finally, a nurse stuck her head in the door and immediately called the attending resident who drew a blood gas. When the numbers came back, Vanessa was already unconscious as they rushed her to the intensive care unit. I followed them down and called Jeff. He was at my sister's trying to get some rest, having been with Vanessa the night before, dealing with the same issues.

In the ICU, they started hyper alimentation after they performed a cut down in her upper chest for another line, separate from the antibiotic line threaded into her port. She was skin and bones. Now they were listening to us, but was it too late? She remained unconscious throughout the day and night. Charlotte wrote the following to Vanessa at this time:

> "I couldn't sleep all night thinking how much I wish I could be with you. I've been sending you positive vibes. I feel your lungs and know they are healing. My lungs are telling yours to breath because we are one. I've always felt that way our whole lives. You are my other half; I need you! Dee Dee, you have the strength of a lion, and I know you will tear through this hard time. I did it last year and now it's your turn. I love you so much. Close your eyes and think of our hearts beating together. We have been through so much and we will get through this. If you get scared and feel alone, remember we are in this together. I can't tell you how much you mean to me because it is a bond that can only be felt between twins. Whatever comes before us, we will always be together because our souls are one!!!"

The following night, while Jeff stayed with Vanessa, I went to my sister's home to get a few hours of sleep. He called me at five in the morning. "You need to come back to the hospital. They are having an early meeting to discuss Vanessa's condition and they want us both there." I threw some clothes on and drove to the hospital.

When we arrived at the meeting, more than twenty interns, residents and staff were already packed into the small room off the ICU. Jeff and I walked over and sat in the only two remaining empty chairs, next to the head of the department.

After a brief summary, he continued. "Vanessa is in a coma and shows no signs of improving. The only option left if she starts to slip into respiratory failure, is to intubate her and place her on life support and then see if she recovers. I've called other cystic fibrosis centers around the country and they all agreed that we should not perform any extreme measures if she goes into respiratory failure, which is also my recommendation. We all need to be realistic about this situation and I don't want to make it any harder than it already is, so if she goes into respiratory failure, I recommend we do nothing to save her."

When he finished, I just looked at him. I was tired and angry. Tired physically, but also tired of not being heard over the past weeks when we knew what she needed and he wasn't listening to her, to us or to his team. I had had it after living in a panic for days on end watching Vanessa struggling to breathe, and now lying in a coma outside the room where we were determining her fate.

"First", I said to him and everyone in the room, "I would like to make it clear that of all the people here, I am one of the most realistic. I have no illusions about the condition of my daughter. Jeff and I might have agreed with your decision if you had done two weeks ago what we asked you to do and what is now being done in the ICU. Vanessa needed calories to give her strength to fight this infection, but you didn't do it. You didn't call her doctors back east to better understand her condition, when I had them standing by to take your call. Now it is too late for all of that, but Jeff and I are not giving up and we are going to give Vanessa a chance to fight. We don't feel she is ready to die yet. If she goes into respiratory failure, we want her intubated and if she does not come out of the coma in two weeks, we will take her off life support. We promise you we don't want her to suffer, but we don't feel she is ready. She needs strength to fight and she is now receiving it. She needs a chance. It is up to her now."

There was absolute silence in the room. Jeff and I were telling the head of the department he was wrong and that did not sit well in these hallowed halls. When we left the room, many of the interns and residents who were taking care of Vanessa came up to us and said, "Congratulations, it was the right thing to do." They agreed he was wrong in postponing her treatment and it saddened me that they had to come to us afterwards to say we were doing the right thing. It was obvious they could not speak up in front of their teacher and mentor. It just wasn't done, but it didn't help Vanessa.

I felt the physician in charge was wrong then and I still feel the same way now. Being a good physician requires many traits and listening to a patient, diagnostic skills, intuition, and compassion are critical when practicing medicine. Communication is key in all illnesses, but especially in a chronic illness, because it is usually long term and changes can be subtle, at times known only to the patient. Working as a team to make this journey as gentle as possible is all we ask as patients and caregivers.

So we made our stand and waited. It was now up to Vanessa. We were lucky not to be alone in this fight and we had help from an expert, caring staff, especially the respiratory therapists who stayed by her side trying to keep the carbon dioxide levels from building up in her body and her delicate lungs from giving out. We also prayed. While everyone kept working and hopeful, she lay silent for another three days.

On the third night, all of a sudden she started moving and soon opened her eyes. At first she looked confused seeing her bed surrounded by caregivers she didn't know with huge smiles on their faces, but then a smile appeared as she asked everyone, "What happened?"

In a few days, she began to gain some strength and was moved at the end of the week from the ICU to the twelfth floor where she gained a little more weight before the intravenous line, providing the nutrients to keep her alive, was removed from her chest. We were then told, that like Charlotte she would need a stomach tube to supplement her meager appetite.

When the x-rays for surgery came back, they showed that her liver was so large it extended across her entire abdomen, making the upcoming surgery more complicated. While Charlotte had remained awake during her procedure, Vanessa would need general anesthesia, a much bigger risk with her low lung capacity. We discussed whether to go ahead, but realized there really wasn't a choice; she couldn't survive without supplemental feeding.

Again, we stood vigil outside the surgical suite for another tense couple of hours until the surgeon emerged from the operating room and announced. "She did well, she's a fighter."

In the recovery room, as soon as she was conscious, Vanessa asked the surgeon if coughing hard could break open the stitches. "In the ten years I have been inserting feeding tubes, no patient has broken the stitches due to coughing." Easily said, but Vanessa had no trouble believing otherwise. Throughout her life, if the doctor said there was no chance something could occur, it would happen to Vanessa. It was our own sick joke.

That night, Vanessa had a bout of coughing. When she caught her breath, she looked up. "Mom, the stitches popped." When the surgeon examined the area in the morning, he said, "You're right, the stitches ruptured. I have never seen it happen before. We will have to see how it heals." The wound never did heal properly and for the rest of her life, she had to deal with the constant oozing and rawness surrounding the tube in her abdomen.

Amidst all of these setbacks, Thanksgiving came and we all had something to be thankful for: Vanessa came home from the hospital.

She was so happy to be home, able to sleep in her own bed and sit in her stuffed purple chair in the living room, content to be back with Darius. But things were different now for both Charlotte and Vanessa.

To step into each day was becoming more and more difficult. Attached to oxygen twenty-four hours a day, needing therapies and medicines throughout the day to stay alive, this became their life. There wasn't much time left for many fun things. We tried to stay in each moment and enjoy what we could, but the "good times" were becoming rare. They were losing what they always cherished, their independence, as they struggled to breathe the abundant air all around them.

☙❧

I prayed to take their pain into my body and live it for them, but I knew that only they could go through this. I asked myself what was I supposed to learn from this as we tried to cope and give strength to one another. Keeping focused on the moment and what could be done now to make things easier in their lives helped me deal with the insanity of it all. To sit and question why or how this could happen doesn't help, especially if you are the person who is living every day with the illness. The only thing I could do was to be there, love them, and try to quell their fears and loneliness.

I began to let myself see there would come a time when Charlotte and Vanessa would not have the strength to work their magic and pull through these crises by sheer will. Eventually, they would lose; we all would lose, but it was too much right now to question what the future held when our hands were full dealing with each day. We had to keep our strength, our sanity and our humor, and believe me whenever we could find a moment of laughter we went there wholeheartedly. It was usually the girls who could find it amidst the daily routine and it was always welcome. They took after their dad on that one.

Knowing all of this did not mean I lost hope. I could so easily have gone to that place of sadness and stayed there, but I consciously chose not to. This was something I could control in an uncontrollable world, trying to stay focused on each day, enjoying the good moments we had each day and on some days, there were still many.

⊘⊘

When I flew out to California in December, I brought Christmas Eve dinner with me on the plane: homemade pierogies, made with my mom over the weekend, and kielbasa, from our local butcher, hoping I could entice the girls with one of their favorite meals. Jeff came out a week later for the holidays and we spent Christmas with the girls' newfound families. Little did we know that this would be the last Christmas we all would share together.

Perhaps the girls knew, because this was the Christmas that Charlotte and Vanessa bought me a very special present. They were so excited when they handed me the box. "We searched everywhere for just the right present and we found it in a little gallery where everything is made by local artists. We hope you like it."

The delicately hammered gold bracelet with two small raised pearls was perfect. The pearls slid and touched one another as I put it

137

on. Once on my wrist, the pearls slid back and rested two inches apart;
Charlotte and Vanessa, separate yet together. I put the bracelet on and
never took it off.

We celebrated New Year's Eve together, sharing the pink pepper-
mint pig Vanessa brought to the festivities. We put the candy pig in the
red velvet pouch and each of us took the little hammer and broke off a
piece to eat. It was supposed to bring us luck in the coming year.

Chapter 31

Charlotte, Caleb

"It has gotten harder lately since Vanessa and I have been so sick. We are their only children and I feel my parents' pain too. They have to watch us go through this and because they were always able to keep us healthy, I think it's hard for them to accept that they can't and they keep thinking they can somehow change this. It is hard for them to watch Vanessa and me go through this at the same time because Vanessa and I are both pretty much at the same point in our disease. But it's difficult to explain because on the other hand, our family has everything we've ever wanted."

Charlotte

A s Jeff and I drove to the airport on January 3rd 1999, for our flight home, I was more anxious than usual about leaving. I was always apprehensive when leaving them, but this time it was more than that. I kept second-guessing my decision to leave. After we checked in for the flight, I called the girls one more time and they assured me for the umpteenth time that it was okay; they were fine.

After arriving home, we settled back in to our routine of calling the girls several times a day. They liked that we each had our own time to talk and they especially liked their early afternoon talks with their dad.

Four days later, we received a frantic call from Darius. "Vanessa is in the intensive care unit in a coma and the doctors don't think she will regain consciousness. She was taken by ambulance to Marin General Hospital because the paramedics didn't think she would make it to the hospital in San Francisco."

Jeff and I were on the last flight out of Philadelphia, each of us silent, our tightly clasped hands the only connection between us.

We arrived in the Intensive Care unit at midnight. Darius, his mom and dad, my sister and Ross, Stephanie and Ian her fiancé, who was a paramedic and heard the call come in, were all standing silently around the bed. In the midst of it was Vanessa looking lost in the middle of an enormous bed with tubes and wires coming out in all directions. The beeps, buzzers, and clicking sounds from the medical equipment filled all the quiet spaces.

About an hour after we arrived, the nurse we had spoken to on the phone at the airport in Pennsylvania came into the room and asked if she could speak to us. Darius, and his mother Debbie, Jeff and I slowly followed her down the hall into a small conference room.

"There is very little hope that Vanessa will come out of this coma; she is losing her battle with this infection. I wish there was something more we could do, but it is up to Vanessa now."

She left and as she closed the door behind her, all the air in the room seemed to be sucked out with her. No one said a thing; we just stared at one another dazed, as we tried to comprehend what she had said. Silently, I laid my head on Jeff's shoulder and collapsed into his arms, welcoming the tears.

When we returned to the ICU, the doors on the other side of the unit suddenly flew open and there was Charlotte, coming through with Caleb at her side. Her eyes were red and swollen and she didn't look well. By morning, she was admitted to the critical care unit two floors directly above Vanessa's room in the ICU.

We met with the hospital's pulmonary specialists, Dr. Nisam and Dr. Margolin, who would become Charlotte and Vanessa's doctors for the rest of their lives. I immediately took a liking to them the first time we discussed the girls' treatment and they expressed their interest in a team effort.

By evening, I had a glimpse of that team approach. It was very late and Dr. Margolin and I were going over Vanessa's chart. I saw the amount of insulin prescribed and thought it was too low. I hesitated because of the newness of the relationship, but then forged ahead when I remembered our discussion that morning. I told him Vanessa's diabetes was very hard to control, especially when she was sick and what had been prescribed looked too low to me.

He turned and looked at me for a while and I must admit thinking he would respond with "I am the expert here," as I had sometimes heard in the past, but instead he smiled and said, "You know her body so well, I will defer to what you think would be the appropriate dose." Wow, was this refreshing to hear. Within minutes, the order was written in the chart and carried out. This remarkable team approach helped us through the rest of the girls' lives with doctors who listened and discussed concerns and ideas and considered them important in their care.

When we talked that morning about the antibiotics the girls needed, I said we had been told they were available only at the medical center in the city. Dr. Nisam asked what they were and said he would have them by that afternoon, and he did. I liked this man.

ॐ

While Vanessa silently fought the raging infection inside her lungs, I talked to her as I brushed her hair or sat holding her hand. Her fingers were bruised and bloody from being stuck every fifteen minutes for a blood sugar reading and I couldn't help thinking she would be mad as a hornet when she came out of this coma; if she came out of this coma. The only time she moved was when we changed her position so she would not get bedsores and I realized, here is my daughter, again fighting for her life.

Several times a day, I made my journey from the second floor to the fourth floor to see Charlotte. Jeff usually stayed with Charlotte to keep her company. They played a lot of gin rummy, and most of the time Charlotte would beat her dad's pants off.

Charlotte and Dr. Nisam took an immediate liking to one another and within a week she was moved from the critical care unit to a regular room. The following Saturday, he came in with his family on his day off to read to his wife and children the books Charlotte and Vanessa had written.

Charlotte was so proud that he took an interest in who she was and not just in her illness. The nurses said that after he met Charlotte and as the year progressed, they noticed Dr. Nisam became more open and communicated more with his patients. We were lucky to have found two compassionate, highly qualified doctors who cared so much for Charlotte and Vanessa. It meant the world to us.

After five long days, Vanessa stirred and opened her eyes. The mixture of antibiotics the doctors and the hospital lab had concocted was working and after another few days, she started feeling stronger and even a little spunky. She wrote the following in her journal. "I remember when I was in the ICU and they didn't think I would live. My mom said that we would always be together, no matter what happens; I will always be there with her. It was hard to hear her trying to deal with it."

∾⳩

One morning, after she had been moved to the critical care unit, I was lying with her on the bed when out of the blue she blurted out, "I am really frustrated trying to decide who to give all my shoes to." Now Vanessa loved her shoes and had a closet full of them to prove it, many never worn, so for her this was a dilemma, although the statement took me totally by surprise. "I'm a ten so forget me," I said as we sat thinking about who wore a size seven shoe.

Not more than a minute later, in walked Stephanie. Vanessa and I looked at each other and laughed. "Stephanie, what size shoe do you wear?" She looked puzzled at the question being asked the minute she walked through the door. "I wear a size seven." Vanessa breathed a sigh of relief. "Stephanie, when I die, I want you to have all of my shoes." Stephanie stood completely still, not knowing what to say or how to react.

She was smiling at the same time tears were welling up in her eyes. I understood completely, overwhelmed by so many feelings myself; happy Vanessa had come up with a solution, devastated as to why.

Vanessa was always dead honest with herself and everyone around her; it was just hard to get used to sometimes.

For over a week, while Vanessa had been in the coma, I slept on a cot in a small room next to the ICU. Now that she had regained consciousness and Charlotte was doing better, Jeff returned home to Pennsylvania. He received this note in the mail a few days later.

> *Dear Dad,*
>
> *The last year has been hard and I don't think I would have gotten through it without you holding my hand. I know I would not have come through the ICU without my daddy by my side rooting for me. No matter what happens, I want you to know you and mom gave me a great life and the love I have for you will live forever. You are not just my dad, but my friend. I love you. When I think of you I get warm inside from the joy you bring to me in my life.*
>
> *Love Always,*
> *Vanessa, "Dee Dee"*

☙�’

I started going home at night to my sister's house after the girls fell asleep, as I had when they were first hospitalized fifteen years ago. Late at night, driving alone along the winding road to the tip of Tiburon released me from the day. With the windows wide open, the cold salty air rushed over me as I listened to opera, loud enough to drown out my thoughts, many nights singing along at the top of my lungs, trying to release some of the pain locked so tightly inside me.

Halfway home, coming up over a rise in the road, I would see the city of San Francisco sparkling in the distance and on some nights, the moon reflected across the entire bay, following me all the way to my sister's.

Stepping out of the car, I would lean over and smell the jasmine cascading over the fence before heading to the deck for some air and a look at the nighttime sky over Angel Island. Soon after, I would crawl into the welcoming bed, trying to fall asleep listening to the waves lapping against the wooden pilings with the sounds of the foghorn in the distance, a soothing balm to my senses.

I looked forward to this routine each night, and each night it overwhelmed me. How could I feel such pleasure and such utter sadness at the same time? My emotions were scratched raw, and there was little time for insight or reflection, which probably was an unconscious choice. Was I really ready for the answers?

As the girls recovered they were moved into the same hospital room, just like when they were seven years old. It worked out well because the room was huge, we could open the windows for fresh air and they had each other for company. Caleb and Darius would arrive after work and because Caleb worked close by, he sometimes stopped in for lunch. We usually all ate dinner in the room, with sushi as the choice most nights.

It was during this hospital stay that I contacted the Center for Attitudinal Healing. A few months before, we had talked about the organization, which provides support for the terminally ill, and although the girls were interested, they had never gotten around to calling. We decided it was time.

On the phone, the director, Cheryl Shohan, explained the various services they provided, including group meetings, volunteer visits to the home and a hospital visitation program. Their volunteers were thoroughly trained to offer support to families dealing with life threatening illnesses, helping them through the fear and uncertainty surrounding their lives at a difficult time. The program is based on compassion and love, bringing kindness and connection to patients and their families.

Cheryl said she would stop by the hospital after work that evening to meet us. She later revealed to me that her first thought as she hung up the phone was that it would be a difficult night, knowing the girls' situation. But her apprehension eased when she approached the room and heard laughter coming from behind the door. When she knocked and opened it, we were all sitting on Charlotte's bed playing cards. That night marked the beginning of our friendship and the miraculous journey with the Center.

When Cheryl was leaving, we made plans to meet at my sister's house the next day and it proved to be an interesting visit. When I opened the door in the morning to greet her, Cheryl was standing there laughing. "You are not going to believe this, but this is the house

Jerry Jampolsky, the founder of the Attitudinal Healing Center, lived in when he wrote the book *Letting Go of Fear*. Would you believe the center was started right here? The meetings and workshops were conducted on that front deck overlooking Angel Island, including the workshops that Elizabeth Kubler-Ross presented. She actually stayed in this house when she was in California and is a good friend of mine."

I was amazed by what Cheryl was telling me, but actually, it made perfect sense. Stepping through the door of my sister's house the very first time, I had been overwhelmed by a feeling of peace and comfort. This house had always been a sanctuary for me. So in a way, I wasn't surprised at all by the connection. I love the way our experiences with one another are woven in and out, the way we are open to influence and help along the way. Those are the riches of life.

ॐ

As we sat on the deck, I knew the Center would play an important role for all of us in the coming year.

Chapter 32

Vanessa

"It's been tough lately. I'm so used to being able to do things and I can't do them now. I am in and out of the hospital. I was lucky because I was healthy when I was young, but it is a slow process. You just don't wake up one day and die, you wake up each day and feel a little sicker, and a little sicker, and a little sicker. The tough part is knowing that it is not going to get any better anymore. But that's life, everyone has their hardship, whether it is living to be 98 and never being in love or living to 24 and having to deal with CF. You learn to cope. You learn to live."

Vanessa

*L*ater that week in the hospital room, the phone rang while we were putting together a puzzle on Charlotte's bed. It was Brooke, Charlotte's best friend from Pepperdine. After some chitchat, Brooke said her dad had seen the girls' books and he wanted to help publish his favorite, *65 Roses.* He envisioned it as a hardbound coffee table book.

Charlotte's face lit up while Vanessa listened intently, trying to contain her excitement. The call sparked smiles all day long as our conversation turned to planning a trip to Denver, where Brooke's father lived and where they would work with the designer on a few of the paintings that needed to be modified for a large scale book. I hadn't seen them so excited in a long time. What a difference one phone call had made.

After much deliberation, we chose a date a month away and worked out the logistics. It was decided that Charlotte would go first and see how things went. It was complicated enough for me to arrange all the necessary equipment and medicines for one, but for both girls to go with no one to take care of them other than Brooke, was just too much. So Charlotte's flight was booked and she worked towards getting physically stronger.

Finally, they both went home from the hospital and every night, with no complaints, Charlotte did her stomach tube feeding, which now required medicine to counteract the constant nausea, all her IV's and medications and four respiratory treatments. She had a goal.

The day came for her to leave and I arrived early to get her ready. I had already shipped ahead her medicines, oxygen, cases of tube feeding, bags to put it in, and diabetes testing equipment, since she too had now developed diabetes, and all her mists and portable nebulizer.

When I walked into her apartment, I immediately could tell she was not feeling well. The thermometer showed she had a slight fever, but that was common now, and she was extremely nauseous.

By now, the high calorie tube feed mixture running into her stomach all night frequently made her throw up, and all the medications she was on just made the problem worse. I handed her the morning pills with a glass of water, including the anti nausea drug, as she started her respiratory treatments. I quietly mentioned several times that I didn't think she should go to Denver as she sat in her chair, her nebulizer in her mouth. "Maybe you should wait until you're feeling better?"

After several tries, Charlotte finally turned and looked at me with tears in her eyes and said in a firm, sad voice, "Mom, if I don't go now, I never will. I must do this or I will have nothing more to look forward to." Looking at her I knew I could not say no, just as I could not say no when she wanted to go to school in California. I couldn't take away the small chance of hope of living her life; I knew she needed to do this no matter how hard it was for me.

Caleb then walked through the door from work, saw the situation and knew that Charlotte's mind was made up, so we reluctantly drove to the airport. As we helped her through the terminal, I felt like running away and hiding. Instead, I sadly watched her determination and will as she accomplished the small feat of slowly walking onto the plane. Caleb and I helped her to settle her into her seat, removing her own oxygen cannula, which was hooked to her portable machine and switching it to the airline's oxygen. I proceeded with all of the steps without comment, but inside, I could not believe I was letting her do this.

Caleb and I waited until the plane took off and then called Brooke to say she was on her way. I also let her know that Charlotte was not feeling well. Brooke said not to worry, she and her husband, Travis, would be waiting at the airport with the oxygen I had ordered and there were plenty of oxygen tanks back at the house for her weeklong stay. Caleb and I had a quick bite to eat and kept saying to one another throughout the conversation that at least it was a short flight; little solace for what we were feeling inside.

Charlotte called after she got settled that night and said she was okay, but I could tell from her voice that she was struggling to convince herself and me all was well. All night I lay awake hoping and praying that Charlotte would be able to enjoy this little respite. She had been through so much lately and had been so excited planning this trip with the hope of getting her book published. It gave her purpose.

In the very early morning, Brooke called to say that Charlotte hadn't slept much, was very nauseated and having trouble breathing. I could hear the fear in her voice. We discussed that it could be altitude sickness at 5000 feet, but it really didn't matter what the cause was, we needed to get her home. I said I would fly out because she could not travel by herself.

Before I had a chance to call the airline, Brooke called back and said her dad had received permission for Charlotte to fly back on a private corporate jet owned by Tele-Communications, Inc., which could fly at a low altitude to help her with her dangerously low oxygen level. Again, we were grateful that another compassionate person had reached out and touched our lives.

I arrived early at the newly built private terminal next to San Francisco's main airport, too nervous to wait at home in case of traffic and of course, it was clear sailing all the way through. With Charlotte's oxygen in tow, I walked into the comfortable waiting area used for private and corporate travel patrons. I went straight to the desk to ask if the plane had taken off from Denver yet, although I knew it probably hadn't since I was so early. They said for security reasons they were not able to give me information about corporate jets with officers on board. When I explained the situation they said that a plane of that type, not necessarily that plane, had just taken off from Denver airport and was on its way.

I sat down and waited. I had no idea what to expect when Charlotte arrived, too frightened to even think ahead. I just waited, keeping everyone posted by phone as to the situation. The plane finally touched down and I drove the car out onto the runway to meet it. The pilot carried Charlotte off the plane as I thanked everyone for all they did. Charlotte, still tethered to an oxygen tank from the jet, was able to chime in, "Here I was flying for the first time in a private jet and all I did was lay my head back on the pillow and fall fast asleep. What a comment on my life, I can't believe I missed it all."

We drove directly from the airport to the hospital and Charlotte was admitted for yet another round of antibiotics and intensive respiratory therapy. Once again, Dr. Nisam and Dr. Margolin worked closely with the hospital laboratory trying combinations of old and new antibiotics against the girls' growing resistance to all combinations of drugs. This became a mission for them and the laboratory staff, and for now, it seemed to be working. That was all we could ask for.

❧❧

Caleb, Jeff and I felt this trip was a turning point for Charlotte. It was such a defeat for her not to be able to stay with Brooke for that one week. In the past, she always could rally when needed and find the stamina to press forward. She started to realize, as we all were realizing, that she just wasn't able to overcome her deteriorating body anymore. It brought such sadness to her eyes.

We were all faced with the true meaning of living with a chronic illness, a terminal illness, the continual setbacks, never feeling good, never regaining the strength lost before the last hospital stay or bout of sickness, the loss of control over their own bodies, the growing dependence on others for the simplest things, all this when they were in the prime of their lives. It was a profound change for the girls, for all of us; a deepening knowledge of their weakening bodies and the sadness that brought. Now, every day became even more important. If they felt okay that day, it was a good day.

Health is something we take for granted until we don't have it anymore. Most of the time we didn't have time for quiet introspection as we went about the daily routine of caring for the girls both in and out of the hospital, but the inevitable changes that were diminishing our twenty-four year old daughters' lives were all around us.

Chapter 33

Charlotte, Caleb, Vanessa, Darius

"I've lived a really good life. It wasn't until recently that I have gotten a lot sicker and my mom thought it was a good idea for me to come to the Attitudinal Healing Center because it has gotten a lot harder for me. I know I'm very lucky. I've never had to be on oxygen all the time until it changed a few years ago. It's hard to be twenty-four years old and in your house all the time and on oxygen and in the hospital pretty much every month. It's just gotten hard to build a life around that. I have a great husband and sometimes I wonder if it's fair to him because he is only twenty-four too. But we laugh and we joke, we have the best times together. We watch movies and we cook and we do everything we can do for how the situation is now.

"On the one hand I feel luckier than any person in this world because I have such a wonderful life and I have so many people who love me. So many people don't have that. It's just that sometimes I feel frustrated because I'm attached to this oxygen all the time and I can't do the things I used to love to do like dance, and run and exercise, all those things. And I know that I'll probably never do those things again."

Charlotte

One of the bright spots in the girls' lives now was the home and hospital visits Cheryl arranged with the volunteers from the Attitudinal Healing Center. Since each of the girls had at least three volunteers, they had visitors at least three times a week. They also tried to go to meetings at the center when they were feeling up to it, but that wasn't very often.

The volunteers brought hope and joy into the girls' lives, carrying pieces of their outside lives into their now circumscribed world. Linda, a volunteer, said of her visits with Charlotte, "Looking forward to what she could do now and doing it without self pity, with such a positive attitude, that is such an important lesson and beautiful gift for all of us to be around." The deep relationships the girls formed with these generous volunteers became as important in their lives as their medical care.

In the spring of 1999, Vanessa and I went to a meeting at the Attitudinal Healing Center. Unfortunately, Charlotte was in the hospital so she couldn't attend. Channel 2 News was filming a story about the center and Cheryl asked us to be part of it. They filmed the group meeting in the morning and asked a few of us to stay for some individual interviews in the afternoon with the broadcaster, Bob MacKenzie.

Vanessa was in her glory throughout the whole process. When they finished the interviews, the newscaster decided to focus the piece on Vanessa and asked if it was okay if the crew went to the hospital to interview and film Charlotte. When I called her to see if it was okay, she replied, "Mom, I look a mess, but oh, what the heck. It's for television."

In no time, we cleared all the paperwork with the hospital's public relations department and the crew went over and interviewed Charlotte and me in her room. The girls loved every minute of that day, and again weeks later when the film crew came to their apartments to interview them in their daily routines with Caleb and Darius.

The broadcast aired in May on the 6 o'clock news and again at 11:00 p.m. We all sat on the couch at Charlotte's apartment and watched their story unfold. There were stars in the girls' eyes when they introduced the segment and by the end of it, there were tears in mine. A few days later, the broadcaster called to say the viewers were calling the station in record numbers saying how moved they were by their story.

A few weeks after the broadcast, Charlotte and Vanessa received a call from Matthew Mitchell, a documentary filmmaker. He had heard about them through Cheryl at the Attitudinal Healing Center and was filming a series called "Which Doctor", about living with a terminal illness. He asked the girls if they would like to participate in the series. He did not have to repeat the question. They were ecstatic.

On a sparkling day in May, Matthew and a correspondent, along with the camera crew, spent more than eight hours filming at my sister's house in Tiburon. It was a long day for Caleb and Darius, but an even longer one for the girls as they rode a roller coaster of emotions, answering questions about their childhood, about cystic fibrosis, finding true love, and now living each day knowing they were dying. But, from beginning to end, it was obvious that they loved every minute of it, telling their story while sharing insight into their lives and what the illness had taught them. Jeff and I were once again amazed, humbled and enlightened by their candor.

Months later, Matthew told us that at the time of filming, he and his wife, Debra, who was there for the entire day, were going through a hard time, but meeting the girls influenced and changed their lives and their marriage grew stronger.

Chapter 34

Charlotte, Caleb

"The hardest part about my illness is that I am the happiest I've ever been in my whole life—yet I am the sickest. It is almost like a trade. It's as if my angel came down and made my life as happy as possible, but then I have this illness we are living with every day."

Charlotte

By now, I was traveling back and forth from Philadelphia to be with the girls as much as possible, staying at my sister's while helping out during the day with intravenous antibiotics, respiratory treatments, and meals, basically anything they needed while Caleb and Darius were at work.

Charlotte was again hospitalized in June, but came home after a few weeks, so I stayed on to help with her therapy and keep her company during the day. Most days I picked up Vanessa to spend the afternoon with us until Darius came home.

I flew home on June 23rd for our twenty-fifth wedding anniversary. We didn't plan anything; just being together was enough, but a special gift was in the making.

When I touched down that evening in Philadelphia, Jeff was waiting at the airport with welcoming arms. On the way home he said, "You're not going to believe this, but mama cactus"—that's what we called her—"has twenty-five buds ready to open. It's unbelievable."

Mama cactus had been given to us more than twenty years before and never had one flower before we moved to our house in Phoenixville, where there was lots of sun on the back deck. Before now, the most flowers mama ever had were eight at one time, so this truly was a very special present.

When we arrived home, we immediately went out on the deck and there stood mama cactus in all her glory, twenty-five enormous white flowers had opened just in time to celebrate our twenty-five years together. The flowers would last for only one night.

❧

On Monday afternoon, a few days after celebrating our anniversary, the phone rang in my office at work. It was Caleb. I glanced at the clock, it was two-thirty my time, eleven-thirty his. Caleb softly said, "I left work at ten this morning to check on Charlotte and found her in a coma, she was not responsive. I called the ambulance and we rushed her to the hospital. Dr. Nisam thinks she will live only another hour or two because her vital signs are so bad."

"We'll be there. Please tell her we are on our way," was all I could say.

I stood frozen for a moment after hanging up the phone, trying to gather my thoughts. I called Jeff at work to let him know, but only got his answering machine, so I left a frantic message saying I would pick him up. Carol, my assistant, gathered my things and said she would keep trying Jeff as I grabbed my keys and ran to my car.

Jeff was outside his office talking to a colleague when I drove into the parking lot. He knew by the look on my face that he didn't have to ask what was wrong. A few minutes later, we were racing to the airport to see if we could get on the last direct flight to San Francisco.

Again, USAirways came through and even told us that when they called to verify this was a medical emergency the hospital said Charlotte was still holding on. When we arrived at the San Francisco Airport, my sister had a car waiting and before we even asked, the driver relayed the same message.

158

When we reached the hospital, we rushed through the hallway to Charlotte's room. The lights were low and Ashnie, a volunteer from the Attitudinal Healing Center, was seated next to Charlotte's bed, reading softly to her. Charlotte seemed aware of us when we leaned down to kiss her.

Over the next few days, Charlotte remained very weak and drifted in and out of consciousness. Jeff and I slept in the room and visitors were frequent. Her favorite music played softly in the background, along with her ever-present cricket machine, which chirped on the nightstand next to her bed while she drifted. The machine played many sounds, including ocean waves and streams, but Charlotte always liked the crickets— she said they reminded her of the days on the farm when she would fall asleep with the sound of the crickets coming through her open window. She also said it helped drown out the sound of her breathing.

We continued to keep the lights low and filled the room with her favorite pictures and orchids—surrounding her with things she loved. We called family and some of her friends to let them know the situation. Brooke told us she was flying out from Denver and Aunt Barbara, who had always kept in touch with Charlotte through the years with visits, letters and phone calls, was coming too. These contacts meant so much to both girls—being sick is so isolating. People don't realize what it means to hear from those who are living a regular life in the outside world. It gives them a little respite from their situation for a while.

After a few days, Charlotte began responding more to her surroundings and talking some. She told us that she knew she was dying in the emergency room, but when she heard Caleb say that we were coming, she consciously decided to stay. I later read this in the writings she kept:

> "It was so soft in the light. I felt as though I was floating on a bed of feathers, kissed a soft yellow. All around are whispers of people that I know. I don't understand what is being said, only that I feel tremendous peace. But it was love that brought me back to life and made me want to stay."

❧❧

We discussed starting her tube feeding again because she was losing weight quickly and needed all she had to fight this infection. She made a face when we mentioned it to her. "I'm nauseated all the time now and just tired of it all." I understood completely and thought we should allow her to go for a few days without it so she could have some peace. But Charlotte relinquished when Caleb and her dad asked her to try once more; the compromise was if she could not tolerate it, it would be stopped immediately.

Three hours after she was hooked up to the feeding tube she became sick. We stopped the flow into her stomach. The look of pain on Charlotte's face said it all. She wanted no more of this.

On Wednesday evening, the night before Brooke's arrival, Charlotte spent almost eight hours with Linda from the Attitudinal Healing Center, dictating nineteen letters to family and friends, asking Linda to distribute them to everyone after she died. The letter to be read at her memorial service was written that night.

ॐ

Thursday was a turning point for Charlotte when Brooke, her best friend, arrived early in the morning from Denver, leaving Garret, her newborn son, at home with her mom and her husband. She stayed by Charlotte's side all day. Towards evening, Barbara, my sister-in-law from Pennsylvania, came through the door smiling. Charlotte had a good day.

Thursday evening, after everyone had gone to get some sleep at Caleb's moms' house, I curled up next to Charlotte on her bed. She told me she was tired. "Half of me wants to go, mom, and half of me wants to stay. I don't want to leave Caleb alone. I love him so much; he's my angel. I'm afraid of what is going to happen to him. I don't want to leave Vanessa, daddy and you. I am so happy now and excited to be with everyone again. It is like a party having everyone here. I want it to stay just like this." It felt so good to feel her joy and I agreed wholeheartedly, I wanted it to stay just like this too.

Friday turned into another good day. By late morning, Charlotte was sitting up in bed with Brooke by her side, even managing a few sips of soup. Laughter drifted from the room throughout the day, bringing smiles to us all.

As night approached, Charlotte looked tired, but happy. She told me as we snuggled in bed that night, "Mom, I made up my mind to stay awhile longer—I want to spend my first wedding anniversary with Caleb. That's my goal." And I believed her.

Brooke left on Saturday to get back to her newborn son, and Charlotte slept most of the day. On Sunday, her Aunt Barbara left, and Patty, Lois' daughter, flew up for the day from Los Angeles to give her a pedicure and manicure. Charlotte rallied for her visit. The morning was tough, as it always was, but she grew stronger as Patty pampered her and talked about what was happening in her life. When Patty was ready to go, Charlotte looked tired and weak.

But as the days went by, she again amazed us with her fortitude, and once again, slowly regained some of her strength. We started the preparations for her to go home from the hospital on home care, only this time she left in a wheelchair, tethered to an oxygen tank and more IV's. At home, she needed a portable commode next to her bed—after weeks of lying in bed, she did not have the strength to walk to the bathroom.

Her mind and heart were determined to live, but we all knew now that her body was growing weaker. The love that brought her back to life was strong, but her body was failing.

૭ᐸ৬

I arrived back in Philadelphia on the red eye once Charlotte was settled back at home. That morning, on my way to work, I noticed the distinctive bright red call of the raspberry on the side of the road. I called Jeff and asked if he would like to go raspberry picking with me after work. We could surprise the girls with their favorite, fresh raspberries.

Jeff brought two large, plastic containers and each of us went off on the quiet road to pick berries. After filling the containers just full enough so the berries would not roll around, but not too full to squash them, we drove to the Federal Express office and shipped them off for overnight delivery.

I waited until the afternoon to call the girls to see how they liked their surprise. Charlotte said they were great, it reminded her of days on the farm. Vanessa, on the other hand, always the teller of truths, said they arrived all broken apart into tiny beads resting in their juices, ready to be made into raspberry jam, although she thanked us again and again for the effort. I called Charlotte back and told her I had spoken to Vanessa and she said, "Yes, my berries were the same, but I didn't want tell you and make you feel bad." That was so typical of them, dead honesty from Vanessa and Charlotte trying to be protective of our feelings, each having its own rewards.

✑✎

As Charlotte promised, her first wedding anniversary came on August 16, 1999 and by sheer will, she was there to celebrate it. Ashnie and I arrived at Charlotte's apartment in the morning and then drove over to the farmer's market early to pick up Charlotte's favorite foods and flowers for their special dinner; she was not strong enough to go out to celebrate at a restaurant so we decided to bring the restaurant to them. Lobster was the requested fare so I picked up extra large tails on the way back to her apartment.

When Ashnie returned later in the afternoon she brought a wonderful surprise, an exact replica of the top layer of Charlotte's wedding cake. It was crowned in flowers and looked just like the picture she had seen.

Meanwhile, Charlotte slept while we set the table with a linen tablecloth and napkins. White roses and purple lisianthus, her wedding flowers, graced the center of the table.

Ashnie and I started dinner. When Charlotte woke up from her nap, I helped her into the shower, the door left open so the steam, which made it hard for her to breath, could escape. She settled onto her shower chair attached to the fifty-foot long oxygen cord turned to the highest setting and she still was struggling to breathe. I helped her out of the shower, but she needed to sit down and rest before I started drying her. "Mom, it is so hard. I can't even take a shower or bath anymore without help, two things I always loved to do. I'm getting so tired."

She sat down on the toilet seat. Charlotte was five foot seven inches tall and now weighed 80 pounds. This was her first wedding anniversary and I wanted to be happy for her, but sadness lay all around the edges. I struggled to keep from crying as I dried her emaciated body.

We chose a long silk nightgown she had received as a gift at her bridal shower but had never worn—Charlotte was a boxer shorts type of woman. She was exhausted but smiling as we looked in the mirror

162

while I brushed her hair. She had made it to her anniversary, riding rising waves of sadness, entwined delicately with joy.

✑✎

When Caleb came home from work, we all toasted their one-year anniversary with champagne. Ashnie and I set out the food and then left for them to enjoy their time together.

When I came in the next morning to see how Charlotte was doing, most of the food was in the refrigerator, covered and uneaten. When Caleb first met her, she could eat so much it even impressed him. Now when we asked her to eat just a little more she would say how much she missed being hungry and how hard it was to eat even a little bit when she had no appetite at all. We understood what she was saying; we just couldn't help ourselves to want more.

Chapter 35

Pat, Charlotte

"I like to make people happy but I see my disease making people sad; that is the hardest part. When they see me struggling, I want them to know that I've had so much happiness and have had a great life and I'm really at peace with everything. The hardest part is I'm not sad I'm going to die, I'm sad the way my life is right now; I can't do the things I love to do. I have always had so many friends around me and I was always busy doing something. Now I feel so sick that I don't even want to write or do my watercolors anymore or even get out of bed because I feel like I have the flu all the time and can't breathe, but deep down, I'm still happy for the life I have lived."

Charlotte

I flew back to Philadelphia for a few weeks in August to catch up at work. In September, I decided to go out to California to spend some time with the girls when they were home and not in a crisis situation. I again stayed at my sister's while she was away with Ross in Nantucket. A semblance of peace always settled over me whenever I walked through their door, no matter what I was facing at the moment. Their home was my sanctuary.

The next day, I gathered up Charlotte and all her machines and medicines and brought her over to stay with me, since she did not get out much anymore. I thought she might like a change of scenery. Each day I drove over to Vanessa's and after all of her morning medicines and therapies were done, brought her over to be with us for the day.

For ten days, we put together puzzles, worked together on a large needlepoint of Millet's painting "The Gleaners," watched movies and talked. It was a very special time. Every day was important and if it was a good one, it is something cherished now. Even in our lives, knowing what lay 'ahead for us, we had taken days for granted; we couldn't anymore.

One late afternoon, Charlotte and I were sitting on the couch together working on a puzzle. She looked at me and said softly, "I really miss going to sleepovers, just staying up into the night, not hooked to machines. I wish I could feel okay just once to do that again, but I know it can't be like that anymore."

I leaned over and held her in my arms, feeling helpless. I was her mom and couldn't even grant her one healthy day, one healthy hour, or one healthy minute to do as she pleased and feel like a normal young woman. All I could say was that I wished we could have done more the past week during her stay with me. "It's okay, mom. It's exactly what I wanted to do, just be together. I really don't have the energy anymore to get out and do things."

She was right. If we took walks, she was in her wheelchair. Sometimes she didn't mind, other times she did. It bothered her when people stared. "People look at you differently in a wheelchair. When I use to walk around with my oxygen, especially when I coughed, they would look scared to be around me, like they were going to catch something. Now that I am in a wheelchair, they don't look scared anymore; they just feel sorry for me."

It was the reason the girls didn't like to go out much anymore. It was a struggle to get up the energy to get ready and go out and then people acted like they were contagious. It's hard for people to understand how it hurts when all they wanted was to be treated like normal human beings.

The last time we all went to the movies together was to see "The Deep Blue Sea", a suspense film about a shark. We were walking down

166

the street, me in the middle, their oxygen tanks flung across my shoulders, the girls attached on either side by trailing tubes of oxygen, and we were openly stared at. Although we tried to ignore it, it was hard to see the hurt register on the girls' faces. That was our last time at the movies, something we always loved to do. From then on, we watched movies at home.

There were times now, sitting next to the girls, surrounded by their beeping machines, manacled to their oxygen lines, intravenous antibiotics pumping continuously into their veins, that I felt overwhelmed and wishing and praying, but for what? I actually didn't know anymore.

For the last year and a half, I had been spending most of my time in California with very little sleep, even with the help of a sleeping pill, and sometimes, I didn't know if I could get out of bed and do it all over again each day. I just wanted to hide from what I knew was coming. But then, in the early morning hours, I would think of the girls. Every day, they had to muster up the strength just to breathe, knowing it would never get any better. This horrible disease was overwhelming them, but they still chose to be a part of life; and even though it was not the life they had hoped for, they were doing their best just the same. They found the courage each day to go on, and surprisingly most days with a smile. They could still find those little bits of happiness in their lives each day and savored them. So how could I give up? I couldn't let them down.

They were my mentors on this journey. Their example guided me through the times of crushing thoughts of what was to come. The girls, without their knowing it, gave me the strength to get out of bed, get dressed and begin another day. And some of those days were still magical. This was one of them.

It was late September, one of those gorgeous autumn days, with a light breeze and a warm sun, a day when everything glowed. Charlotte was tucked back in her apartment with Caleb, and I was with her. We had been inside all day so I asked, "How would you like to go for a walk around your complex and maybe we can see the sunset?" Since the wheelchair was not her favorite mode of transportation, she hesitated, but then agreed.

After dinner, we took the elevator down to the first floor, rolled through the hallway and out the door into the warm, sunlit air. "Charlotte, I've never been up on the fire trail, how about it?" I said.

"Sure", she replied, "we can try it, but it's really steep." Neither of us had been up there, but it was an adventure and at this point we needed a challenge other than curbing her growing weakness.

I pushed her around the bend and started up the hill, not too bad, and around the next curve. Wow! Up ahead was a long, steep incline. "Straight up to the top, we can do it," I said as we pushed ahead.

Halfway up the hill I was drenched in sweat, loudly panting, and my heart was pounding against my chest, looking for a way to either escape or burst. I stopped and turned the chair sideways, fearing the breaks wouldn't hold. "Are you okay?" she asked. "Sure," I gasped, seriously wondering if I really could have a heart attack before we made it up to the top. But after a short rest, we continued to climb.

Finally, we reached the top and stopped so I could catch my breath for the third time. The road narrowed onto a dirt path, which led to a fence with a small metal gate. Charlotte got out of the wheelchair and walked through the gate as I collapsed the chair and quickly squeezed past, getting her settled once again. It was getting late but we were determined to make it to the top and see the sun set over San Francisco Bay.

The path soon leveled off and although it was a bit bumpy for Charlotte, it was easier for me to push and we started to relax a little, able to open ourselves up to the surrounding beauty and smells and it was heavenly. The warm air was filled with the scent of wild rosemary and sage, intermingled with the heady aroma of eucalyptus, reminding me of the fragrant incense in church, only this was untamed and pure.

The sun was just nearing the horizon as we stopped to face the west. Intoxicated by the sweet dense air, we watched in silence as the sun disappeared into the horizon on the Bay, flashing a blaze of pinks, purples and egg yolk yellows throughout the sky. Not wanting to break the spell, we waited a little while longer, until a chill started to fill the air. I reluctantly turned Charlotte's chair around and we headed home.

As I pushed the wheelchair back down the path to the road, I started thinking about how steep the hill had been when we came up, and now how in the world was I going to get her back down safely? We managed the gate and in no time we were at the top of the hill. I stopped to consider the best way down. If I went back and forth across the road, maybe we could slowly snake our way down. It seemed logical until

I started diagonally across the road and the wheelchair began to tip downhill. This was not going to work; it was way too steep.

Two women walked by, looking at us as if we were nuts, not too far fetched, and asked if they could help. I said no and immediately regretted it. I couldn't believe I was that stupid, but I wanted this to be for Charlotte and me, no one else. I realized after taking several steps straight down that if I held on tightly, kept my body tipped back, and took one small solidly placed step at a time avoiding all pebbles, I might be able to proceed slowly down.

It took a long time, and we joked as I struggled to keep my footing. "Charlotte, if I lose my grip, try to aim to the road at the bottom that goes uphill, not downhill." As soon as the words were out of my mouth, I realized how absurd it was to think she could actually steer this thing. "Sure mom, I can see it now in the paper, mother takes daughter in a wheelchair on treacherous fire trail, loses her grip as the daughter careens down the steep hill, crashing at the bottom. What was she thinking?" That was exactly what I was wondering to myself as I slowly took the next step, holding on to her for dear life.

When we finally did reach the bottom of that hill we were elated, as if we had accomplished something grand that day. We had many laughs about it later; best of all we had the memory of that sunset with the air filled with wild incense.

Chapter 36

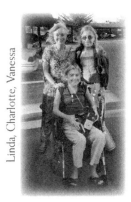

Linda, Charlotte, Vanessa

"It's hard because there is never a time when one isn't sick. Someone is always sick. One gets better; the other one gets sick. That's why it's been so up and down. My poor parents, it's a double whammy. I'm feeling good one day and Charlotte's not feeling good that day. That is just how it is now. When you see how sad they get when you really get sick, you hate knowing that you are causing that sadness and you hate knowing when you are gone they are going to feel just as bad, or worse. But hey, right now I am good so hopefully for the next few months I can stay out of the hospital."

Vanessa

For the last few months of her life, Charlotte didn't leave her apartment much. It was such an effort for her to get around and she seemed more comfortable in her little space, filled with the things she loved. So towards the end of September, when she asked Caleb if they could go to Six Flags for one last roller coaster ride, he was a little more than surprised.

On the following Saturday afternoon, they drove to the amusement park, with wheelchair, oxygen and all. Obviously, they hadn't thought through all the implications before they set out on this adventure. Caleb just wanted to make her happy.

As they climbed into the front seat, they realized she couldn't ride the roller coaster with her oxygen tank because there was no safe place to put it, so they left it with the attendant. Strapped in tightly with bars and belts, off they went. It was a ride neither of them would forget.

She told me later that as soon as the ride started, she thought she was going to die; she couldn't breathe, strapped in so tightly between the bars and belts, with no lifeline of oxygen. "I didn't think I would make it," was all she kept saying when she called me that night. It was an interesting conversation because although I knew she must have been scared stiff when she couldn't breathe, I picked up an excitement in her voice I hadn't heard in awhile. I guess now that it was over, she thought of it as an adventure, something she hadn't had in a long time and in the end she felt like she had accomplished something that day; she had some fun and excitement one more time.

ॐ

October was hard for Charlotte. She was home, but being alone during the day now became a struggle for her. It gave her too much time to think about what she was facing. We tried to be there most of the time, but it was not an easy task. Caleb went home on breaks and for lunch. I was working some from California, but Vanessa also needed help. Attitudinal Healing was a godsend and Charlotte looked forward to their visits from the outside world. Breathing was becoming more and more difficult and it frightened her.

Jeff came out and spent a few weeks with Charlotte and Vanessa, playing cards, helping with medications and running errands. They were happy to have the company and he loved being able to help. Charlotte was experiencing a lot more pain now—she couldn't breathe without her chest hurting. Her whole body ached, especially when she woke up in the morning.

The low dose oral morphine she was taking didn't touch the pain anymore so we arranged to have an acupuncturist and massage therapist come every day, sometimes twice a day if her pain was bad. She grew attached to Debra, the massage therapist, who not only eased some of the pain, but also comforted her each day with her loving touch and kind words. It didn't take away the pain completely, but it helped make it more bearable.

✍️

Vanessa in the meantime went to Yosemite with Darius, his mom and his step dad for a long weekend. Originally, the trip had been planned for the previous year, but they had to cancel when Vanessa was in the hospital for two months. The amount of equipment and medicines now needed to be packed was overwhelming. Vanessa and Darius brought so many tanks of oxygen that their Audi station wagon was having trouble pulling the hills, so they had to stop and transfer some of the tanks into his mom's car. We joked later that they should have opened up the tanks and had their own oxygen bar on the ride home. It was a memorable trip for them all.

> *"I call my portable oxygen tank wimpy because if I tilt him over at all he wimps. I have liquid oxygen at home so I just fill up the portable with the mother load, the main tank. The portable tank weighs a ton. You would think they would come up with something lighter because people with lung conditions are generally weak."*
>
> *Vanessa*

Chapter 37

Charlotte

"I'd like to be the first because I don't think I can deal with having Vanessa die. When you are twins, you feel their pain—it would be too hard. I think we are prepared for it—someone has to go first and I always partied because I wanted to be first in a way. I think that is why. I wanted to be first."

Charlotte

Jeff went back to Pennsylvania at the end of October and I was planning to fly out to California after a long planned retreat for work. The Saturday before, Caleb called and said that Charlotte was having trouble breathing so he had rushed her to the hospital. Throughout the next day, Jeff and I talked to Caleb and a few times to Charlotte on the phone.

She sounded okay and told us not to rush out, but we knew from experience that how she sounded was no gauge as to how she actually was; she never wanted to worry us. In the middle of the day, Jeff and I decided I should fly out first thing Monday morning and forget the retreat; we had a feeling I needed to be there.

When Charlotte and Caleb had moved into their apartment together, they were given a prayer plant, which would become known as ET. It was one of the few plants that had done well in their apartment. For the past year, whenever Charlotte would get sick enough to go into the hospital, the plant would wilt, the leaves would dry up and it would look as if it was going to die, despite the fact that the watering remained the same; Caleb was diligent about that. When Charlotte came home the plant would recover with new leaves; hence the ET connection.

Toward the end of October, the plant started looking bad, and as the days wore on, it continued looking worse.

I flew out early on Monday morning. When I walked into the hospital room, Charlotte gave me a big smile and we hugged for a long time. Caleb was seated in a chair by the side of her bed and Ashnie was reading to her. All day long, Charlotte drifted in and out of consciousness to a place far away, taking flight to places only she could reach.

At one point while we were talking, Charlotte's eyes wandered to a space next to me. She focused her gaze and seemed transfixed, as though listening intently as a big smile lit up her face. Laughing, she said, "Mom, there's a clown standing next to you."

Not quite understanding what was happening, I asked the nurses to reduce her morphine, thinking she might have had too much in her system, hence the drifting in and out of consciousness. It didn't make any difference and the pain she had been experiencing over the past few months did not seem to be overwhelming her now, even with less morphine. Charlotte seemed in a different state. Caleb and I spent the night.

In the meantime, Vanessa was struggling at home. She was coughing up blood again so she was admitted into the room next to Charlotte's the following morning. On a stretcher on her way to x-ray, she asked if they could stop outside Charlotte's room. Charlotte saw her through the open door and they both looked at one another with tears in their eyes. With arms outstretched, Vanessa said "I love you Daw Dee" and Charlotte replied, "I love you Dee Dee." Lately, they were using these childhood names again, when things were sad or difficult.

Later that morning, I stood outside Charlotte's room as Dr. Margolin told me her tests showed she was now harboring a new hospital-borne bacteria that was resistant to all antibiotics and could be transmitted to anyone she came in contact with. It meant that anyone who came into her room had to use a mask, gown and gloves for their own safety. It was just another blow to Charlotte. Now people couldn't freely hug and kiss her, and her sister was told she should not go into her room for fear she would contract the same bacteria due to her compromised immune system.

Caleb and I decided to take our chances; she felt isolated enough without even more barriers to contend with. Vanessa was not well enough to visit so that alleviated the threat to her at the moment.

Later that afternoon, our long time friends, Betsy and Pat, who were identical twins and had been in Los Angeles, decided to fly to San Francisco to see the girls, not knowing all this was happening. They came with lots of hugs and kisses and goodies as they settled in each of the girls' rooms for a visit.

When Charlotte saw the whole box of Tastycake Krimpets, her favorite sweet, she struggled to look excited. We tried to tempt her with a bite, but by the time I opened the packet, she was not even up to a taste. She said it looked good, but couldn't do it. The simple pleasure of eating her favorite snack was gone.

Jeff kept in constant touch and as the day wore on I called to say he needed to come right away; this time it was different. Strange how we had almost gotten used to being told they were dying and then somehow they would pull through, to the amazement of the doctors and nurses and us. I headed back to the room and handed the phone to Charlotte so her dad could tell her he was coming.

On Wednesday morning, Dr. Nisam and I stood outside Charlotte's room after he had been in to see her. With his eyes filled with sadness he said, "I think she is dying, but she has come back so many times, I just can't be sure."

After we talked, he went into Vanessa's room, sat down on her bed and took her hand in his, "Vanessa, I think your sister is dying, I am so sorry." After Vanessa was finished with her therapy, she put on a gown, gloves and mask and walked over to Charlotte's room to spend the day with her, while a steady stream of visitors drifted in and out.

It was a good day as we sat together talking about times at the farm, plays they had put on, walks in the woods, uncontrollable laughter over nothing, all their various pets from dogs to abandoned birds and squirrels, all the memories of our lives together when they were little. Vanessa was so protective of Charlotte the entire day, even while her own body, attached to oxygen and intravenous antibiotics, was failing. We all had some time alone with Charlotte to try and say what was in our hearts. She was awake and aware but had a far away feel about her, as if she were slowly leaving us.

We no longer had the steady stream of nurses and doctors; most of the normal medical routine had been discontinued for her comfort. An IV was still attached to the port in her chest through which fluids flowed to keep her comfortable. Later this was used for morphine to ease her struggling. Her oh-so-thin body was still trying to conduct its routines and she struggled to be lifted onto the commode next to the bed. She wanted to do that right up until she settled into unconsciousness that evening. Where she found the strength, I will never know.

ॐ

Jeff came through the door at about 8:30 that night. A big smile swept across Charlotte's face as he crossed the room to give her a big hug and kiss. He seemed tired and disoriented, not part of the rhythm of the past few days.

A little while later we were standing around the bed and all of a sudden Charlotte said loudly, but almost to herself, "I get it. I get it. It's a joke." She said this several times with an amused look on her face. It was so cute to see her laughing and feeling proud of herself. We all looked at each other, not knowing what it was about. Was it a revelation about life; was it something she was remembering about some past experience? We'll never know, but I have my own theory. I believe that she was talking to that clown she had seen standing next to me on Tuesday, and they were sharing their own private joke. She would have liked that.

As the evening wore on, the sound of the cricket machine and the steady droll of the bi-pap resonated through the room. The bi-pap assisted Charlotte's breathing, pushing oxygen into her lungs through a tight-fitting mask placed over her nose and mouth. It was a delicate balance to keep enough oxygen in her bloodstream without increasing the carbon dioxide to dangerous levels. Both Vanessa and Charlotte had been using the bi-pap for years. In the beginning, it was just used in the hospital at critical times, but lately they not only slept with it on all night, they also used it during the day. It just made their struggle to breathe a little easier.

By 11:30, Charlotte was drifting. "Mom, can you keep talking to me?" and as I nodded yes she turned to Caleb and whispered, "Can you kiss me?" Caleb leaned down to Charlotte and while he kissed her, the sound of crickets from her cricket machine serenaded them. We held her hands and we each whispered I love you, as Charlotte closed her eyes and faintly whispered three times, "I see the color white." It was the last time we would ever hear her voice.

৶৻

Caleb stayed next to Charlotte throughout the night, sitting in a chair by the side of the bed, holding her hands nodding off to sleep for a few minutes at a time. After a few hours, Jeff fell asleep on a bed in the corner of the room. I took off my shoes and got into bed with Charlotte, taking her in my arms and talking softly to her. "Remember in the spring when all of the daffodils were blooming close to the woods and we would pick armfuls of them and bring them into the house, filling the air with their lemony scent. It always meant that summer was just around the corner, your favorite time of year. Can you smell them, Charlotte?"

After drifting into the coma, Charlotte moved very little and didn't seem uncomfortable. At first, I was giving her liquid morphine by mouth, then by syringe through her stomach tube. At 1:30 the nurses hooked up a morphine drip into her port. About 2:30, as I was talking and rubbing her back, she grabbed my arm and started rocking it back and forth. Her grip was so strong I thought she was going to break my arm. All of a sudden, I felt as if she was passing all of her energy into me, saying goodbye. I will never forget the power in her grip and the feeling of her energy flowing through me.

I knew she did not want to go, but I also knew she would this time. In the days and months that followed, I often thought about this moment, hoping it was not a cry that she was scared or in pain. She had told me during our talks together that she didn't want to be scared when she died, or alone, so I tried to hold her tight all night, connected, so she wouldn't be afraid, whispering good thoughts to carry with her.

I woke up Caleb and Jeff to tell them what had just happened, thinking that at any moment Charlotte would die. The steady rise and fall of her chest to the mechanical rhythm of the bi-pap machine was the only movement now; her spirit seemed to have left, leaving her wasted body to go through the rest of the dying process. Over the next few hours, her breathing would stop, I would hold my own breath, and after what seemed like minutes, she would take another breath. By five o'clock her breathing was extremely labored. Her lungs were full of fluid, her breaths shallow and close to the surface, rattling. She was drowning in her own vile mucus.

I woke Caleb and Jeff again, thinking her last breath would be at any moment. As the minutes ticked away, the cricket machine kept up its background chatter. I lay next to Charlotte, while Jeff and Caleb were on either side of the bed, each of us silent, holding onto each breath, talking to her, waiting. She was twenty-four and her body was young. It took a long time to let go.

At 6:11 am, on that morning, Thursday November 11, 1999, Charlotte slowly, deeply inhaled her last breath. As she exhaled, her life flowed past us in a long sigh, each of us saying goodbye and wishing her a good journey. Caleb reached over to the bedside table and turned off her trusted cricket machine, a constant chorus in her house, in the hospital, in her life. Her crickets were forever silenced.

☙❧

I turned off the bi-pap and took off the mask. Charlotte was no longer in need of it. I decided then that when Vanessa's time came, she would not have the bi-pap at the end. Charlotte's face looked stressed from it and I am sure it prolonged the process of dying. I wish I had known that.

Jeff was distraught and kept sobbing, "I can't believe she is gone," and he kept saying no, no, no. It scared me, and I stood silent not knowing what to do. It had happened so very quickly for him since he had only just arrived hours before she died. All we could do now was hold each other. When he settled, I went down the hall to the nurses' station to let her know and she called the doctor. Jeff and I then went to tell Vanessa.

Throughout the night, I thought of Vanessa, lying in the next room, herself so frail. Should we wake her and have her stand vigil with us? We decided against it. We were afraid for her to actually experience her sister's death. It would be too close, seeing what she would be facing. On the other hand, we also knew she would be heartbroken not to be with Charlotte. In the end, we chose not to wake her. We could live with her anger more than the thought of her witnessing Charlotte struggle through the night. I just couldn't imagine it.

When we walked down the hall into Vanessa's room to wake her, we didn't say anything as she opened her eyes, she knew. We watched helplessly as she screamed and fell into our arms. We struggled with her oxygen and IV pole as she scrambled out of bed to rush to her sister's room. She fell onto Charlotte's bed, saying she was sorry she could not give her one last hug.

We called Darius to come. His mom came with him and they took Vanessa to her room while Caleb went home to get clothes for Charlotte. I washed her emaciated body and cut a small piece of her hair. Holding her in my arms, I felt an intense heat emanating from her back. She must have struggled so hard to generate that much heat. I am sorry, Charlotte.

When Caleb returned, he removed Charlotte's engagement ring, a ring he had placed on her finger only a year and a half before, and gave it to me. I wear it with my wedding band, sized from a three and a half to a seven. Amazing how tiny she had become.

As we began to dress her, we realized that the top and bottom he had brought from home didn't match. Caleb and I looked at one another with the same thought: Charlotte would be okay with mismatched pajamas. She was into comfort, not high fashion, and actually would have thought it funny. Vanessa would have been another story.

As we lay her head back down onto the pillows, the struggle of dying showed clearly on her beautiful face.

Through the window I could see the sun was just beginning to rise over the hills, sending out streaks of flaming colors against a sparkling blue sky. A lone deer wandered up the steep slope across the way and although I had spent many days and nights gazing out of that window, it was the first time I had ever seen a deer on that hillside. This was a morning Charlotte would have loved; perhaps it was her gift.

Jeff had gone to call friends and family back east. Drs. Nisam and Margolin came in to say good-bye to Charlotte. Nurses came to console and be consoled; flowers began arriving, even an arrangement from the x-ray department, everyone in the hospital knew the girls. Amidst it all sat Vanessa, next to her sister, receiving everyone with strength and grace.

Later in the day, we called the funeral home and they came to take Charlotte's body away, wrapped in the quilt from Lois, her hands filled with roses. Alone in the room, Jeff and I collapsed into each other's arms.

♌︎☞

The next day we received a condolence call from Bob MacKenzie, the broadcaster from Channel 2 news. He wanted to let us know the station was going to announce Charlotte's passing on the news that evening and would be showing the newscast again because so many were touched by her story.

A few weeks later we received a copy of the broadcast and all the out takes from the interviews. As Jeff and I watched, it was both heartwarming and heartbreaking to see and feel the girls fill the room with their energy and spirit.

Chapter 38

Charlotte

"It is not how many pages your life story holds, but what is written within."

Charlotte

When Charlotte was in a coma and nearly died in July, my sister and I had arranged for the girls' cremations, knowing it would be too overwhelming to deal with when the time came. I wanted to make sure that I and not someone else would be able to take care of their bodies; they had been poked and prodded enough. I brought them into this world and wanted to be the one to take care of them as gently as possible when they left.

I quickly realized the arrangements made months before were just the beginning of the process. But my first priority was Vanessa, who was still in the hospital. Thankfully, Jeff stayed with her while I was running in all directions. I was also lucky that my sister, her husband Ross, and friends helped me arrange the two memorials held on opposite coasts for family and friends.

In the midst of all of this, Vanessa was desperately struggling to cope without Charlotte and although her dad stayed with her at the hospital, she still couldn't sleep. Two days after Charlotte died, Vanessa decided she had to go home; it was too hard to be in the hospital without Charlotte. She came home the next day on intravenous antibiotics and oxygen, trying to settle into a life without her sister.

She and her dad played cards, watched movies and did all of her medicines and therapies, until Darius came home from work. I usually cooked and we all ate together and then Jeff and I would head to my sister's to sleep. We didn't have time to grieve; Vanessa needed to be cared for and comforted in her grieving and I was trying to write obituaries and plan memorials. The grieving would have to come later.

While we had decided months before that we wanted to make the urn for their ashes, it seemed overwhelming now that the time had actually come, but Vanessa, sick as she was, persisted. Jeff, Vanessa, Caleb and I met on a cold night at the pottery studio where Vanessa had made many gifts for friends and family, even the bowls for the kittens she raised. After much deliberation, we picked out a container we thought would be big enough, pleasantly shaped and not too much like a cookie jar, although Charlotte would have loved the idea since she had a sweet tooth like Vanessa and her Nan.

We chose a pale mint green, a color Charlotte looked beautiful in, to glaze the background. Each of us painted a star on the circular lid, four stars, and each one a little different. Then Jeff painted a large orange, yellow and black butterfly, like the ones we released just a year before on her wedding day. Caleb chose to do a bright yellow daffodil and a purple iris, two of her favorite flowers since childhood. I made a pink rose in remembrance of her children's book and all the beautiful roses she had painted over the years.

Jeff continued painting a vine of pale green ivy around the top of the container representing the ivy in her book, 65 Roses, and then added her name and dates. But it was Vanessa's creation that proved to be the "pièce de résistance."

There was Vanessa, crouched over the table, her whole body intently focused as she drew and then painted a unicorn and elephant facing one another, trunk and horn entwined in an embrace, each with a big smile. As far back as I can remember, Vanessa had loved elephants and Charlotte unicorns, so what could be more fitting?

When Jeff went to pay for the urn and paints, the owner said a woman that Vanessa had met earlier in the evening at the pottery studio had already paid the bill in honor of Charlotte. We were again humbled by an act of kindness shown to us through the girls.

On Saturday morning the funeral home called to say that Charlotte's ashes were ready. We picked up Caleb and within twenty minutes were parked outside the imposing, concrete building. An immense set of wooden doors stood at one end of the landscaped path, one door slightly ajar, inviting us into a peaceful, contemplative hall, a dramatic change from the chilling façade.

Mr. Craft was there to greet us as we passed through the sunlit, orchid-laden hallway to his office. On his desk was a box, twelve inches square, wrapped in fine white paper, with a round gold seal on top. We all stood there looking at this small package on his desk, not knowing what to say or do. He understood and gave us time.

After awhile, Caleb went over to the desk, picked up the box and carried it outside and into the heady scent of eucalyptus. "Charlotte is much heavier than I thought she would be. I always knew she had bigger bones than Vanessa, but I never thought she would be this heavy," Caleb commented as we walked to the car. With that said, he passed the box to Jeff and then to me. We all agreed. "I hope her ashes fit in the urn; this box is a lot bigger." We drove home without a word, deep in our own thoughts.

Entering his apartment, Caleb walked over and placed the white box on Charlotte's favorite chair. He pulled her pale green cashmere blanket from the back of the sofa and carefully draped it around her ashes before going into the bedroom for the small pillow she slept with each night, and placed it by her side. Charlotte was home.

∂℞

I woke up the following Thursday thinking of Charlotte, as I did every morning. The clock said six eleven; the exact time we had turned off the cricket machine only one week ago.

That evening, friends and family gathered to celebrate Charlotte's life at the home of Linda, who had worked with Charlotte through The Center for Attitudinal Healing. There was good food, good wine and a chocolate cake for Charlotte's and Vanessa's upcoming birthday. I tried my best.

During the evening Linda read the letter Charlotte had written for her memorial service. She explained how the letters had come about and distributed the pale pink envelopes, our names carefully written on each one, to those of us who were there. At the end of the evening, we all gathered in the backyard to remember Charlotte by releasing white balloons into a midnight sky. After letting go of hers, Vanessa gazed up into the sky for a very long time.

Charlotte's ashes remained on her lounge chair until the night before her memorial service. Christine, who brought light and laughter into the last nine months of Charlotte's life through The Center for Attitudinal Healing, invited us to her home on San Francisco Bay to place Charlotte's ashes into the urn. Only weeks before, Charlotte and Caleb had been there for a lobster and champagne dinner, and although Charlotte couldn't eat much, it meant the world to her. It was to be her last outing.

As Vanessa, Jeff and I were getting out of the car, Caleb pulled up. Walking over, I glanced at the passenger seat and there sat the white box; the seat belt strapped tightly around it. I could only smile and knew Charlotte would be smiling too.

At Christine's, we toasted Charlotte with a glass of wine and opened the box. Resting in a heavy clear plastic bag, the ashes filled the box halfway. Caleb lifted out the bag and placed it in the urn; the ashes fit and still had a long way to travel.

A little while later, he picked up the urn, put it into the box and closed it up. At this point, there was nothing more to say or do so we said our goodbyes; it was too much to fathom what we were actually doing there.

Chapter 39

Charlotte

"As the days slowly passed, the flower felt a sadness building. Deep down she knew that her time would be short in this world that she loved. 'Let your beauty shine and brighten the world around you,' said the old oak. "Just then a loving hand lifted the little flower up into the world. She wanted to stay, but knew she must go."

65 Roses

*I*t was a magnificent, crystal clear day, a Charlotte kind of day, as we gathered for Charlotte's memorial in the small, circular sanctuary at the San Francisco Seminary in Corte Madera. The sun shone through the stained glass windows, creating patterns of light on the walls throughout the room. Charlotte's wedding flowers graced the table next to her urn along with a picture from her honeymoon in Hawaii.

Chris Davis presided over the service. Over the past year, he had become a close friend to the girls through his hospital ministry, bringing much comfort and humor into their lives. They shared many common interests, including a love of sweets, especially Nutter Butters. He knew the girls always had a stash of goodies in the drawers next to their beds, so his hospital and home visits generally included snacking; even when the girls did not partake anymore, they still kept them on hand for him.

The time came for me to read the letter Charlotte had written for her memorial. Stumbling a few times, I began:

"To All My Family and Friends Who Have Loved Me and Whom I've Loved"

I was born into this world with Luck, surrounded by support and Love. I've lived such a full Life, full of Joy and Happiness—something few people experience.

All of your Love has shielded me from any pain my illness may have caused and I am forever grateful.

Even though I have been sick for most of my life, I never felt sick because you all allowed me to have such a normal life. I treasure this Gift.

When I think of you all, I think of what a charmed life I have lived. So many feelings, so many memories come flooding in as I think of all of you, that words cannot express. In this room is so much Love and I am here with you holding your hands.

Thank you for teaching me how to live each day to the fullest.

Love is the most important thing in Life to have. Therefore, I die a rich woman, filled and overflowing with so much love.

Everyone in this room is part of the greatness and Peace that I feel right now.

You have been such Angels to me and now it's my turn to be your Angel, watching over and protecting you—cheering you on to be the happiest you can be and live the richest, most love-filled life you can imagine.

Remember to imagine. Imagination is the key. Imagine how wonderful your life can be. Even in the hard times, remember that with Love you can always pull through.

And I will be sending all of you Love and Healing from wherever my journey takes me on the Grand Adventure of Life and Living.

All my love, Charlotte, July 1999

Reading this letter at both memorials was one of the hardest things I have ever had to do. But I did it for Vanessa, who was sitting in the front row, watching me, helping me. She needed to see me do it. When I sat back down next to her, she squeezed my hand.

After a minute, she stood up with Darius at her side and walked slowly to the podium, tethered to the oxygen tank on Darius' shoulder. In a strong, but tired voice, she recited a poem she had written for Charlotte, her intermittent cough echoing through the hushed church. "And to my other half where ever she be, you were but a better half of me," was how the poem ended. I still don't know where she found the strength.

Some people got up during the service to talk about Charlotte; Dr. Nisam was one of them. He said that although he never spoke at memorials, he wanted to today. "I caught glimpses of two young ladies who have filled their cups to the brim with love and with life. Their lives were dedicated to living and not to dying, but it has been the constant reminder of the fragility of their lives that has pushed them and their family to the fullest. When Charlotte was so sick and in pain she still had a smile when I would walk into the room and always asked how my family was. I will always remember what a courageous person she was— never before has a patient touched me in this way."

Chapter 40

Vanessa, Charlotte

*"When I came to this life, I was blessed with a wonderful twin sister.
You have been through everything with me, the happiest of times and
the saddest of times. You are my soul sister. God gave you to me to
understand all that we go through. I'm at peace now watching over you.
Love, your other half."*

Charlotte

On November twenty-seventh, Jeff and I flew home to prepare for the service in Pennsylvania. I mention the date because when we arrived home and I went out back for some air, I couldn't believe my eyes; all of my roses were in bloom. This was the end of November, this shouldn't be happening.

In the morning, I cut each and every flower. The colors—deep pink, coral, fuchsia, lemon yellow, and raspberry red—were sublime as I spread the hundreds of petals on the floor of Charlotte's room to dry. She would have liked that.

The night before the service, Vanessa, Caleb, Darius, Jeff and I gathered in our living room to place Charlotte's ashes into the urn. On the bottom we laid a colorful butterfly magnet given to us by Christine. Caleb poured in her ashes before we placed the rose petals and her wedding flower on top.

We each then went upstairs to get a glow-in-the-dark star and comet from her ceiling. For many years this universe of planets, moons and stars, pinpoints of pale green light, surrounded her as we turned out the lights when she went to bed. They were still glowing as we closed the lid—Jeff sealing it with melted wax.

The urn spent one last night at home with us, on the mantle, next to Charlotte's photograph. We did discuss the idea of not burying it, not wanting to let her go, but in the end, we realized she had to be next to my dad, near the farm she loved, just as she wanted. It was just so hard to do.

On December fifth, at least three hundred people flowed through the doors of St. Peter's church, high up on the hill in Chester Springs. It was a California type of day, sunny and in the seventies, unusual for this time of year, but appropriate.

Vanessa flew in with Darius two days before, on December 3, her 25th birthday—struggling to breathe and find some semblance of living. She now stood inside the church doors, Darius by her side, the slender tube of her oxygen tank connecting them. She greeted each and every person who came through the doors for well over an hour and a half. From their faces I could see that her physical condition and incredible endurance were heartbreaking for them.

After I read Charlotte's letter, even harder this time, Vanessa took the podium. She remained strong while reading her poem for Charlotte, but when she had finished, Darius had to help her back to her seat.

As he had in California, Jeff spoke about Charlotte, capturing her spirit in his words:

> "Charlotte loved the movie Titanic. She knew the iceberg was looming ahead, but continued to live and love. She knew her illness was ultimately going to end her life, but she did not let that stop her from living a full life, without bitterness. Charlotte always followed the sun and since it rises in the east and sets in the west, that is how her life went, bringing the sun, like today, into our lives. She packed a lot into the years she had."

Our friend Michael Bacon played "Unchained Melody" on the cello and the music resonated throughout the church and penetrated into our bodies. Halfway through, a beam of sunlight pierced the stained glass window, enveloping only him in a warm peaceful light. Everyone noticed it when we talked about it later, commenting that it made the hair stand up on the back of their necks. We all agreed that our first thought when it happened was that Charlotte was making her presence known.

After the service, a line of people streamed across the country road to the cemetery, Caleb leading the way holding Charlotte's urn. In the small grave next to my dad, we scattered the dried rose petals across the bottom, creating a soft, colorful cushion in the cold dark earth. Kneeling, I placed the urn in the center and filled all the empty spaces with roses until it was ablaze with color.

After the graveside service, Vanessa moved closer to peer in while softly saying, "Dirt. Charlotte liked to play in the dirt. We used to run though this cemetery and play cemetery tag, and of course she always won." A quiet laughter filled the air.

The memorial reception was held at Pat and Ray Jones' house, where only fifteen months before, Charlotte and Caleb had been married; the circle of life.

We had ordered a birthday cake with Charlotte and Vanessa's names written on top, in honor of Vanessa's birthday and in memory of Charlotte. I thought since many of our friends were there, it would be nice for Vanessa to celebrate, since she had been traveling home to Pennsylvania for Charlotte's memorial on her actual birthday.

When it came time to cut the cake, everyone gathered around Vanessa as I tried to explain. "I know this may seem strange, but I wanted to be able to celebrate Vanessa's birthday with everyone here. Vanessa is now twenty-five, a milestone. I guess we won't be singing happy birthday because of the circumstances, but I will leave that entirely up to Vanessa." As I turned to her, she promptly replied in true Vanessa form, "It sounds like a good idea to me," and with that everyone started laughing. As we sang happy birthday, Vanessa included Charlotte in the refrain. When the cake was cut, Charlotte's side of the cake remained untouched.

The ride home from Pat's home was quiet, each of us absorbed in our own thoughts. Vanessa broke the silence from the back of the car.

"So many people loved Charlotte. I really don't think that many people will come to my memorial."

For a few moments, none of us knew what to say; it was such a raw and honest statement, pure Vanessa. Gathering our thoughts, we said she would have just as many, if not more, and tried to convince her of that, but as silence settled over us again, the impact of her statement hit me. We had just buried Charlotte and here I was talking to Vanessa about her imminent death and how many people would be coming to her memorial.

All I could do, as I had done over and over through the years—was to focus on what needed to be done for her when we arrived home. Tomorrow would come soon enough.

Chapter 41

Vanessa, Darius

"Darius is everything. He is my best friend. He has stood by me through thick and thin, no matter what happens he gives me hope and makes me look forward to tomorrow. He gives me a reason to get up in the morning and makes my life easier too. He helps me with all of my medications. He is a very special person."

Vanessa

We celebrated Vanessa's birthday a week after Charlotte's memorial. Her birthday dinner of lobster and champagne at Betsy and Michael's house in the country was the same menu and same place as for the girls' twenty-first birthday. All the same people were around the table, only this time there was one empty chair.

How strange to celebrate Vanessa's birthday without, in the same breath, celebrating Charlotte's, but we did, with an unspoken sadness. When we sang Happy Birthday, Charlotte was included in the refrain. I couldn't help but wonder what Vanessa was thinking that night, her first birthday without Charlotte by her side. She never said.

Vanessa was scheduled to leave for California with Darius and his mom and step dad a few days after the service, but she was exhausted and needed some time to rest and gain strength before the flight home. I decided to fly back with her the week before Christmas; Jeff would follow later in the week.

It took us weeks to get some control over Vanessa's diabetes; her highs and lows were dramatically increasing. She would seem okay one minute and then drop to dangerous lows the next minute. She couldn't be left alone because we never knew when she would have one of these sudden blackouts and she wasn't steady on her feet anymore.

Two weeks before she was supposed to go back to California, she fell out of bed. Which was becoming increasingly common. She broke a small bone in her foot. "Just another battle wound," she commented, vowing a little broken bone wouldn't stop her from getting back to California for Christmas.

At night, Jeff usually went to bed and I stayed up with Vanessa until she finished her last round of antibiotics for the evening. It was a quiet time when we could talk and this was how I found out why Charlotte was so afraid and so angry at us and at life, after we moved from the farm. The reason still haunts me.

Vanessa and I were sitting upstairs on her bed talking about the move and how hard it was for them, when they were just becoming teenagers and experiencing more symptoms of their illness. I told Vanessa I had tried talking to Charlotte about it later, but Charlotte told me she really didn't remember much about that time in her life, it really wasn't who she was. She had blocked it out and now she didn't want to even think about it. She was so adamant, I didn't keep asking.

Vanessa sat listening with her head down and was quiet for a long time as I watched her from the opposite end of the bed; something was very wrong when Vanessa had to search for words. She slowly looked up and stared straight at me. "Mom, Charlotte was raped in tenth grade. She would never tell anyone and that was why she was acting so crazy. She never wanted anyone to know because of all that had happened to us."

I don't remember what I said to Vanessa. I guess, like Charlotte, I didn't want to admit to myself that something so horrible had happened to my daughter. I could not comprehend that Charlotte had to carry that burden with her through the rest of her short life. We had moved two innocent young girls to a place where they had to grow up instantly and I will always have to live with that. I just hope she really was able to hide the scars deeply enough so she didn't ever think about the episode again, but I doubt it.

Chapter 42

Vanessa, Darius

"When you fall in love with someone, you can't help but stay with them no matter what. When we first dated, I was really healthy, so it really wasn't much of an issue back then. It wasn't until the last two years that I've gotten really sick, but he puts up with it. And Darius gets to see the self-pity part, poor guy. I'm not always up every second of the day, everyone has their moments, and he allows that. Darius makes me feel like a normal woman, a twenty-four year old. Hey, I do have CF but oh well. I am still a normal person living a life. I am still here."

Vanessa

A s the days passed, Vanessa grew quieter, more introspective, especially when we talked of her love for Darius and the life they had made for themselves in California. Several times she told me she wasn't ready to die and she continued to make plans for the future, determined to will the inevitable away.

So, with that spirit in mind, I decided, "Why not?" It had worked before and we certainly all wanted to believe, so just like the lion in the

Wizard of Oz, one of their favorite movies, I kept saying. "I do believe, I do believe, I do, I do, I do."

But when I allowed myself to look closely, I realized that the forceful conviction Vanessa once had was gone. In her eyes I could see she had lost some of the hope that somehow, someway, things would all be okay. Not saying anything, she started preparing in little ways; we all started preparing in little ways.

✑✌

For twenty-five years our lives revolved around both Charlotte and Vanessa, almost as a single entity because with identical twins, what you did for one, you did for the other; they liked their equal time. Now that Charlotte had died, things were very different.

We found in the last years of their lives that spending time with each of them became harder as their health deteriorated and they needed more care. It was a dilemma caring for Charlotte at her apartment while I was worried about Vanessa alone during the day in hers. So usually I would run back and forth, which made it difficult to find the little moments of joy, which we desperately needed in the over-riding weight of sadness and responsibility.

Now, with all of our time devoted to Vanessa, it felt odd. We had never thought of one without the other. But Vanessa thrived on it. Her personality actually changed. It was uncanny, but somehow she took on some of Charlotte's attributes, becoming more open, softer, more affectionate, qualities she always had but that were somewhat overshadowed by Charlotte. Maybe this time alone with us for Vanessa was a gift from her sister.

Chapter 43

Vanessa, Pat

"When you realize you don't have that much time left, you tend to treasure each day more and more, which is good, because you can lose someone and say I wish I did that, I wish I said that; we know it can happen so we express ourselves more."

Vanessa

*I*n the middle of December, my friends at work gave Vanessa and me a gift certificate to a spa in Philadelphia so we could spend some time together. It was a very kind gesture, but it was hard for us to find the enthusiasm for it. Yet we decided to make the effort and Jeff drove us down to Philadelphia and dropped us off at the front door of the spa.

When we went in to change, I had to take off the bracelet the girls had given me and leave it in my purse in the locker, which upset me because I forgot to leave it at home. So it was not a great start. We tried to relax and go with the flow, but it wasn't easy, especially since Vanessa couldn't be without oxygen, so that limited what she could do. To be honest, at this point it took a lot of effort just to get up in the morning, never mind find pleasure in anything.

But we tried to make the best of it. By the time we were ready to leave, Vanessa's oxygen tank was almost on empty and her blood sugar was running low, so we rushed through checkout to get to the car where Jeff was waiting with another full tank of oxygen. On the way home, we stopped to get Vanessa something to eat so she wouldn't pass out.

After settling Vanessa at home with all her mists and medications, I noticed my bare wrist and went over to my purse to retrieve the bracelet. Looking through my purse again and again, all of a sudden it hit me; it wasn't there. Retracing my steps, I realized the only place it could have been lost was at the desk when I pulled out my wallet to pay, so concerned with Vanessa running out of oxygen, I must not have seen it fall to the floor.

I felt sick. How could I lose the very last gift from the girls? Running to the phone, I called the spa. It was closed so I left a detailed message and called the corporate offices again and again, week after week, offering rewards, writing letters, whatever I could do. Weeks went by but I never heard a word and never found the bracelet.

When Vanessa and I went back out to California for the holidays, we went to the shop where they had purchased the bracelet. The sales person contacted the artist who said it could be replicated for $350. I thanked her, but at this time we could not afford it; there were too many other pressing expenses. But every time I looked at my wrist, it was a reminder of what I had lost.

In February, I ordered the bracelet; it didn't matter whether we could afford it or not. I decided I wanted Vanessa to know it was replaced.

About ten days after I had purchased it, Jeff called from Pennsylvania to say the bracelet had arrived. Enclosed with the box was a letter from the sales person who fondly remembered meeting the girls when they bought the original one. She wanted us to know she had credited our credit card and that she had paid for the bracelet in honor of Charlotte and Vanessa. I could not believe it. This was another brief encounter with the girls, yet one that left such a deep impression.

✍

But wait, the saga of the bracelet didn't end there. It continued on after the girls had both died. One night after gardening all day, I sat down on the couch to read and noticed that one of the pearls in the bracelet had fallen out. Jumping up, I found a flashlight and ran outside to search the garden, nothing; scoured the house, nothing. After awhile it dawned on me; what was I thinking, the pearl was tiny; it was a lost cause.

I didn't sleep well and early the next morning I asked the girls to help me find it. Then, while going into the bedroom after my morning walk, I stepped on a tiny pebble with my bare foot. Reaching down to brush it off, I saw that it wasn't the pebble. It was the pearl. Looking up and smiling, I thanked the girls; little did I know they still were not through.

✍

In March of 2004, Jeff and I used frequent flyer miles and Marriott points to celebrate our 30th wedding anniversary in Paris, France. It was a trip we never thought we would be able to make. In Paris, we walked from morning till night, seeing every part of the city, the buildings as impressive as the art within them. We were enchanted.

One late afternoon, upon returning to the hotel, I plopped myself down on the bed and while taking off my coat, saw that my bracelet was missing. Immediately, I felt sick to my stomach. It could be anywhere, but all I could remember was taking off a pair of Vanessa's gloves when we entered the Museum d'Orsay; maybe it slipped off with them. It was a long shot, but with me distraught, Jeff rushed down to the hotel desk and asked them to call the museum. "No, no bracelet had been found."

How could I lose my most precious piece of jewelry, twice—especially when I never lose jewelry? After hours of self-accusation, suddenly a peace came over me. I understood that maybe it just wasn't meant for me to keep these bracelets, losing one in Philadelphia, a place the girls considered home, and the other in Paris; a city we all had hoped to visit, leaving something special of ourselves in both places. Releasing them was a way I could let go and hope that whoever found them felt their significance.

I decided not to replace the bracelet this time; it just didn't feel right—the girls are always with me, bracelet or not.

Chapter 44

Vanessa

"As long as I have today, everything is looking up. Some people don't have today."

Vanessa

By the middle of December, all our hard work paid off. Vanessa was looking and feeling stronger so we began packing for California. Her diabetes was somewhat under control and we worked out her tube feeding so she wouldn't get sick to her stomach; one can of formula, spaced throughout the day, which I slowly injected into her stomach tube with a huge syringe, but only if she was up to it. This way she did not wake up in the morning with the intense nausea after five cans had been pumped into her stomach all night.

I did a little Christmas shopping for her, since she tired easily now and we didn't want her exposed to any colds or flu. Several times, Jeff took her to the ceramics studio after work so she could make some Christmas gifts for family, friends and of course her cat Sabastiani, a bowl she decorated with paw prints. We opened our gifts the night before leaving for California and saw how busy she had been.

For her dad, a wooden wine holder, with two hand-painted tiles, one for white and one for red; a perfect gift with his interest in wine. My first package was a rectangular picture frame encircled with hand painted flowers for the thousands of pictures Jeff had taken through the years. As I opened the second carefully wrapped package, the first thing I saw was a radiant sun painted on the lid of a small, white rectangular box. On one side of the box, it said, "I love you" in bold black letters. On the opposite side, "Vanessa Lynn Robbins, December 1999." I could no longer hold back my tears as I contemplated the meaning of those words and how hard it must have been for Vanessa to paint them. The words seemed so final.

✄ఴ

We left the next day for California. Vanessa stayed busy on the plane writing out Christmas cards as I relayed the addresses to her and sealed the envelopes. She was very productive and looked happy to have accomplished her task by the time we were ready to touch down in San Francisco.

That uneventful trip holds good memories for me. We were just a regular mom and daughter traveling together, involved in everyday things. There was no feeling of panic for those few hours; it all felt so comfortable, almost normal, something I hadn't felt in years. Only the oxygen she was attached to revealed the truth of the situation.

✄ఴ

Darius was at the gate to greet us, smiling, Vanessa's portable oxygen tank, filled to the brim, slung over his shoulder. Vanessa beamed when she saw him and stayed wrapped in his arms for a long time.

On the way home, he told us all about the Christmas tree he had bought. "When I walked into the Christmas tree lot, this scrawny little tree was propped up all by itself in the far corner. It looked so lonesome; I had to buy it." Vanessa just smiled, happy to be home and with Darius again.

When we walked through the door of the apartment, the scent of pine filled the air, making it finally seem like Christmas. I am a believer in smells and the impact they have on our lives, and the scent of fresh-cut pine meant Christmas to the girls and to me.

Every year when we went to cut that special tree, first we had to smell it so that we would pick the most fragrant. Of course, many we chose based on fragrance never lived up to that first spicy whiff of pine once they were inside and decorated, but this tree lived up to all expectations.

Vanessa and Darius named it the Charley Brown Christmas tree. It was small and a little crooked, but when dressed up in all its finery, nothing could match it. The intoxicating smell of pine only increased in time because Vanessa needed the house kept very warm and as the tree dried, the scent grew stronger. Whenever passing by, I leaned in close to inhale that magical smell. Darius had chosen just the right one.

Chapter 45

Vanessa, Darius

"My family and friends have made me optimistic about life by having their support and love. Why live life and be a grouch? Yes, I get sad and depressed and I usually get it out and then move on. Yes, I get upset sometimes about my life, but then I sit and put my head down and think that for every second I am sitting here feeling sad and upset and depressed, I could be sitting here doing something worthwhile. Time is way to precious and so my attitude changes really fast."

Vanessa

J eff arrived in California a week before Christmas, and one day we decided to take Vanessa and Stephanie to Petaluma, a little town known for its thrift and antique shops. This was going to be a Vanessa kind of day.

Vanessa had always been the ultimate shopper. She could find a bargain anywhere, especially when browsing in thrift or antique shops, honing in on that special something as if she had radar. I on the other hand, have never been a shopper.

For a long time, she had been looking for a particular ring to give to Darius and today she was determined to find it.

She asked the saleswoman if they had any rings. "Not like the one you described, but there is a jewelry store going out of business a few streets up that may have one."

Vanessa's eyes lit up. We scooted out the door as quickly as Vanessa could manage, but not before she purchased a pair of earrings she had spotted. Then she hotfooted it up the block, as fast as her little body would carry her, attached to her dad by the tube from the oxygen tank. She looked so cute in hot pursuit of a bargain.

We entered the tiny shop, which had been in business for over fifty years but now was closing because the owner's husband had died recently. As soon as we walked through the door, Vanessa spotted the ring in an almost empty display case. Asking to see it, she could barely contain her excitement. After examining it as only Vanessa could do, she proclaimed this was the one. But she was not ready to pay just yet; there were more bargains to be had.

We perused the cases and at seventy-five percent off, everything became open for consideration. Vanessa bought Stephanie a gold ring engraved with tiny delicate roses, a ring Stephanie wears every day now. Without Jeff knowing, Vanessa also bought a silver penknife and had "To Dad, Love Vanessa" engraved on it. She gave it to him for Christmas. I bought a baby silver comb and brush set for a future time and couldn't resist the single pearl necklace for Stephanie and a thin gold band to wear with my wedding ring to remember this day. It feels good next to Charlotte's engagement ring. All in all, it was a good day.

Vanessa was all smiles when she gave Darius the ring on Christmas day—and he in turn surprised her with an engagement ring, something she had always wished for. She was so proud as she held out the delicate diamond band on her hand for us to see.

Vanessa, Darius and Debbie, his mom, and Bill, his stepdad, spent Christmas Day with Debbie's sister, and her family. It was a long day for Vanessa and on the ride back home, she said she was so tired but still had to do all of her IV's, hours of mists and therapy before going to bed. Darius suggested that maybe she shouldn't do them all that night because it was late. Vanessa replied softly from the back of the car, "If people only knew how lucky they were to just come home at night, brush their teeth and crawl into bed. I would love to have just one night when I could do that again. How nice it would be."

When she got home, tired as she was, she still did all of her meds and mists. That was Vanessa.

ঔ৲

During the holidays we decided that Vanessa needed something to look forward to, so we planned a trip to Hawaii. Vanessa, Darius, Debbie, Bill, Jeff and I would all go. Jeff, Vanessa and I had never been there and Vanessa had always dreamed of going, especially since Charlotte had been there twice and loved every minute of it.

After much deliberation, we booked a trip for nine days at the Four Seasons on the big Island of Hawaii, leaving April 6, 2000. Vanessa reserved the rooms, complete with an outdoor garden shower facing the ocean. The place looked fabulous. She was so excited; we all were excited.

Chapter 46

Vanessa

"Whatever is good I try to focus on now and I try to filter out the bad. I just try to live today for today. It's all anyone really has."

Vanessa

In February, Vanessa's strength and determination started to wane, but for Valentine's Day, she and Darius went to the Post Ranch Inn in Big Sur for a long weekend, compliments of her Aunt Janice and Uncle Ross.

She wasn't feeling well, but was determined to go. Except for a flat tire on the highway, the rest of the trip was uneventful, if you call uneventful lugging a car full of medicines and oxygen to stay for a weekend. But they were grateful for the change of scenery and some time away together in a beautiful place.

They cuddled up in their room in front of the fire for most of their stay; it was such an effort to go out anymore. In any case, it rained most of the weekend anyway.

When Vanessa returned, her cough was worse and again was tinged with blood. She checked into the hospital, determined to get better, with one goal and one goal only, to go to Hawaii on April 6. So with this incentive, she entered the hospital and started her routine IV antibiotics, respiratory treatments, and twenty-four hour tube feeding because she was so very thin and frail, and intense monitoring of her blood sugar. Her diabetes needed to be regulated again so we started all over with her numbers and finally got it under control, which helped her state of mind too. The highs and lows can make you cranky and disoriented. I flew out to California a few days after she entered the hospital and my sister sent flowers from Hawaii to spur her on. We had all the nurses and doctors talking about her upcoming trip and she was motivated.

Darius' mom and stepdad often stopped by, Bill bringing one of the playful poems he had written for Vanessa, which always brought a smile to her face. It became the duel of competing poems. Bill would bring one for Vanessa and if she didn't have one in return, she made it up on the spot. Vanessa loved it; Bill loved it; we all loved it. It was such a relief to laugh over something silly.

A few times when she was in the hospital, her room faced Bill and Debbie's home in the hills. Every night at a certain time they would flash their lights to say hello or goodnight and Vanessa would return the greeting. It gave her something to look forward to at the end of her long days in a hospital bed.

Chapter 47

Darius, Vanessa

*"One of the nice things about having a disease where you die slowly—
one of the only nice things—is you get to take the time to be with the
people you love and take the time to tell them. We still plan; we still talk
about the future. When we stop planning then all hope would be lost.
Relationships and friendships, having people around me—that's what
keeps me going, and Darius."*

Vanessa

A s we did on many nights now, Vanessa and I were playing cards
on the hospital bed. She had been silent for a long time before
she finally spoke. "Mom, it feels different this time. My body
feels strong, but my lungs don't feel right, they seem to be breaking
down. I have tried to keep fighting and that is what has brought me back
so many times, but eventually you can't fight any longer. You can't fight
forever; it only lasts so long."

As she spoke, I could see the sadness and fear in her eyes, knowing
she had thought about this a great deal before saying anything. Hearing
the words spoken made me feel helpless and frightened because I was

thinking the same thoughts, I just didn't want to admit it. That was always Vanessa's strength, a raw honesty whether you could bear it or not.

Each day, when I saw how frail and tiny she was in that hospital bed, I could not fathom how she would ever be able to gather the strength to go to Hawaii. We started talking about postponing the trip for a week or two. I said we would wait and see because we could change it at the last minute so she shouldn't worry.

At this point, she needed help to get out of bed to walk, shower or go to the bathroom. Her oxygen levels varied wildly and it was very scary for her, scary for us all. Sometimes when she was gasping for air, we had to place an oxygen mask over her nose cannula to double the amount of oxygen so she could breathe. This helped the immediate panic, but it created a bigger problem; the more oxygen she received, the more carbon dioxide she retained in her body, which eventually leads to coma. It had happened to Vanessa several times before and she had almost died, so they decided to use the bi-pap not just at night while she slept, but also for a time during the day.

Amidst all of this, Vanessa kept saying that she thought she could make it to Hawaii. "I know this is my last trip, mom, but I really want to do this and I think I can." Now Vanessa was the little engine that could and I was still the lion in the *Wizard of Oz* chanting, "I do believe."

When Vanessa woke up on the ninth of March, her right arm was double its normal size. As soon as she saw it, she knew the port embedded in her arm had blown. Most ports are placed in the upper chest by the collarbone, but not Vanessa's. When her veins were too scarred anymore for peripheral or PIC lines, she had insisted the port be put in her arm, not her chest. Why, I will never know because it would have been easier to deal with in her chest, but she was stubborn and we had to choose our battles.

Looking at her arm, she was mad. "Mom, I can't believe it blew now. It should have lasted longer than this." A few minutes later, Dr. Margolin came into the room and Vanessa simply told him as he came over to look at her arm, "I thought for sure when I got this port it would last at least until I died. Even the port won't cooperate." I could see he was a little shaken by her statement, but after regaining his composure he said, "Maybe we can get a rebate on that one." Vanessa looked at him and started laughing. So with her humor restored, they continued their banter. Vanessa could be mad as a hornet one minute, but could let it go the next.

Now we had a decision to make. If Vanessa was to continue fighting, she had to get another port. The peripheral IV's they were using since the port blew only worked for a few hours because the antibiotics were so hard on her scarred veins. We told her the surgery was up to her, because the anesthesia would be very dangerous due to her low oxygen levels and she might not wake up. Calmly, Vanessa made the decision for all of us. "Really, what choice do I have but to go ahead and try?"

∅ৡ

That afternoon, I was down waiting in radiology while Vanessa was having the scans done for her surgery the next morning. An older woman, looking very unhappy, was sitting next to me in a wheelchair. As Vanessa was wheeled from one room to the next, she waved at me from a distance.

A few minutes passed before the woman asked, "Was that your daughter on the stretcher?" "Yes." "What is she doing here, she only looks about fifteen. Why would she be hospitalized?" I laughed. "Don't tell her she looks fifteen, she would not take that lightly. She is twenty-five and is having x-rays for another port to be put in. She has cystic fibrosis." I explained what that was and in the conversation, told the woman that her identical twin sister had died recently of the same disease.

She talked about her children and grandchildren and I told her about the girls and our life together—I don't know why, but it just felt right. Over the short time, her whole demeanor changed and she began smiling. "I guess I'm lucky to have lived such a good life and long enough to see my grandchildren. Thank you for telling me about Charlotte and Vanessa." She was smiling and talking as they wheeled her away for her test.

In the morning before going into surgery, Vanessa met with the anesthesiologist. Sitting on the stretcher, she leaned towards him and said in a very serious voice, "I want you to know I am a very complicated patient." The doctor paused, slightly amused. "I could tell by this three pound file for so young a patient that you certainly are." Vanessa was taken aback for a moment and then smiled along with him before asking him about his medical experience. By the time they were ready to go into the operating room, she seemed very comfortable that he would be the most important person with her during surgery. We each took a few moments with her before she was wheeled away.

It was a long wait, two hours longer than expected. We all jumped up from our seats when the doctor finally came out and said it went well. When we went in to see her there she was, a big smile on her face, sitting up on the stretcher, again astounding us with her resilience and strength.

We had all been so worried that the surgery would not go well, but we should have known. Vanessa tended to come through these big crises well. For her, the challenge was dealing with all the setbacks, the everyday details of trying to keep her body and spirit alive through all the losses.

There was a bright red two-inch scar with a large bruise around where the old port had been; she said it was her battle wound. From what we could see around the bandage on her chest, the new port looked good, but it was beginning to hurt. She requested more Demerol, but was told it was only available on the surgical floors, a big letdown because her everyday aches and pains had disappeared with the Demerol and for a few hours she actually felt good. The alternative they gave her wasn't the same.

During this hospital stay, and especially since Charlotte had died, Vanessa had bouts of coughing up blood. We kept thinking, kept hoping, that it was a polyp or a nose bleed dripping down the back of her throat, anything but what it was, her lungs.

Time after time, Vanessa would cough into a tissue, glance slowly down, examine the contents and then look straight at me, while turning the tissue over to show me the bright red stain. And each time the silence hung between us as we acknowledged through our eyes what it meant.

☙ઽ

Days went by and Vanessa rallied. She was still determined to go to Hawaii and that was what we focused on. At first I really didn't think she could do it, but when I saw her determination, I realized if that was what she wanted maybe somehow she would be able to find the strength.

Her goal became everyone's goal in the hospital and we began working on getting her out of bed, first in a wheelchair and then walking.

Vanessa had a very determined walk. First, she would scan the distant horizon focusing in on her goal, trying to calculate how far away it really was. Then, locking her eyes on the objective, she would move one foot in front of the other in an unsteady gait, as if propelled by some unknown force. She said she had to keep moving in order to live. And in many ways, she was right.

In a few days she was able to walk with help down the hallway of the hospital to the elevator, through the side entrance and out into the California sunshine. Oh how we loved sitting together on that stone bench, feeling the warmth of the sun on our faces, Vanessa attached to her oxygen and her IV pole.

She seemed especially pleased on the day she walked all the way down to the bench without assistance and we sat silently basking in the sun. After a while, she let out a deep sigh. "Mom, my life has changed so much lately. I can't even do the simplest things that most people don't even think are pleasures; the things I took for granted when I was healthy."

After what she had just accomplished, I was surprised by her comment, but by now, the sadness had settled deeply in. We just didn't talk about it much. I took her hand and probably said something to try to make her feel better, but at this point, there was nothing to do except to be there.

Dr. Margolin was standing at the end of the hall smiling when he saw us coming off the elevator. "I'm amazed and excited to see you out of bed and walking down the hall on your own. Vanessa, you always continue to amaze me. I think you are almost ready to go home."

That was what Vanessa wanted to hear—what we all wanted to hear. Everyone was excited, coming in and out of her room to congratulate her.

Chapter 48

Merlin, Darius

"Leaving Darius behind worries me the most because we are best friends. He means the world to me. Sometimes I feel like I don't want to be with him just because it will save him the pain in the end, but he always says let's live today for today, we want to make the best of what we have left. We are still making memories and so if I'm not here someday, in ten years or twenty years or ten days, he will have those memories."

Vanessa

On Monday, March 13, Vanessa was ready to leave the hospital. With everyone rooting for her, with lots of hugs and kisses from the nurses and staff and many requests for postcards from Hawaii, we took Vanessa home.

Usually when she came home from the hospital it took her a day or two to catch up on her sleep and get back into her home routine; this time it was different.

I came over every day to stay with her while Darius went to work. She didn't get out of bed much and when she did it was only to go as far as her overstuffed velvet chair in the living room, where she would do her mist and try to eat a little.

It was hard to rally her out of bed even when new catalogs came in the mail, which she always loved perusing, carefully selecting a few special treasures and then waiting with anticipation for them to arrive in the mail.

The week progressed, but Vanessa was not getting any stronger. She wore the bi-pap machine for longer periods of time. When she did not have it on, her pulse would plummet and she would be gasping for breath. Darius and I were always trying to adjust her oxygen levels so she wasn't struggling to get what little breath her tiny body would take in.

The respiratory therapist started coming every day, monitoring the bi-pap machine and trying to make her more comfortable. Her sputum now was always tinged with thin streaks of blood. It was strange because her diabetes seemed under control and her body seemed to want to continue to fight, but as Vanessa had suspected a month before, her lungs were giving out.

On Thursday, out of the blue, Merlin, Darius' yellow Labrador Retriever, suddenly became ill. Darius' mom called to say that the veterinarian didn't know why, but he was dying and there was nothing they could do. Vanessa and Darius made plans to go over to his mom's that night to say good-bye to him.

I slowly helped Vanessa dress. We did it in stages because it tired her out just to lift her legs to put on her socks and shoes. Finally she was ready. She sat on the couch, elbows on her knees, head in her hands, waiting for Darius to come home from work, looking very pale and tired.

When Darius arrived, she tried to get up to leave, but as she moved unsteadily away from the couch, her eyes filled with tears. "I can't go, I just can't do it. Please give Merlin a big hug and tell him I'm sorry I couldn't be there for him."

Darius left to go to his mom's to say good-bye for both of them. I helped Vanessa get undressed and we sat together while she did her medicines. When I tucked her into bed, I recited our refrain, "Good night, sleep tight, see you in the morning light." "See you later alligator," "After awhile crocodile," we chimed back and forth, harking back to childhood memories at the farm. It made us each smile, but as I kissed her good night, we couldn't speak about what we saw in one another's eyes.

Merlin died on Saturday. It sounds strange but I believe he died for Vanessa; he passed on so he would be there waiting for her, a comforting presence. If Darius could no longer be with her, then a part of him would be.

✣

We had a lot of time to talk that week. It's funny how you want to say profound things, but that is usually not what's most important. One afternoon we were sitting on the couch together and I told her how proud I was of her. "You endured all these years of dealing with diabetes, doing all your daily treatments, even when you were dead tired and just wanted to lay your head on the pillow and fall asleep like everyone else. I always knew you actually took the packets of vitamins and medicines I sent each month trying to keep you healthy. You have always fought so hard to be strong and do all you needed to do, even when your body and mind didn't feel like doing it and you still are trying. Daddy and I are so proud of you." I saw her face light up as I spoke.

Darius told me later that Vanessa was so glad I knew how hard she had worked over the years to stay healthy. Being a twin, she always knew she was more diligent about her medicines than Charlotte was, and for me to recognize it meant so much to her. It's funny that of all the things we talked about, that was one of the most important to her; for Jeff and me to know she tried her best, even through the most trying of times. When I heard how happy it had made her, I only wished I had told her sooner; I always thought she knew.

✣

Vanessa and Darius spent Saturday alone together. I was hoping it was a good sign that they didn't need me there. Early Sunday morning Vanessa called and said she had a very bad night and was coughing up large amounts of blood. I rushed over to talk to them about what to do.

The respiratory therapist came and confirmed that Vanessa was no longer in respiratory distress; she was in respiratory failure. Her lungs were so weak that the bi-pap was actually doing most of the breathing for her, but it only could do it for so long because it was very hard on her damaged lungs.

After he left, I went in to the bedroom to talk to them about what to do. She asked if I would call the hospital and talk to Dr. Margolin, hoping it was a problem in her throat. I knew it wasn't, we all knew it wasn't, but I called. "You can bring her in, but I also think Vanessa is in respiratory failure and the effort to get her to the hospital will only weaken her more. If she wants to die at home as she has said, she may not be able to if she comes in; the journey back and forth would probably be too much. I am so sorry."

I can't recall the thoughts that raced through my mind as I hung up the phone. All I knew was that I had to tell my daughter that she was dying and there was nothing we could do.

When I walked into the bedroom and faced Vanessa and Darius, I didn't know what to say, but I could tell from their expressions that they already knew what their options were. I left the room so they could be alone to decide what they wanted to do.

Chapter 49

Vanessa, kittens

"What is hard for me is that I want to be there to help my parents and Darius through it all and it's so hard knowing I'm not going to be there to give them the hug they need or the kiss they need or hold their hand when they need it. That's what is the hardest. That I won't be there to do that."

Vanessa

Vanessa decided that afternoon that she wanted to die at home. I contacted hospice and by the next day, we were initiated into the program. Since hospice used a different insurance provider, everything had to be switched to a different carrier. This was very stressful for us all. The oxygen tanks, medical supplies such as IV solutions and respiratory machines, medicines and therapists had to be switched. That meant all the previous equipment had to be moved out of the house and all new moved in, IV poles and all. It was very disturbing to Vanessa, who was very weak and very tired.

After all was said and done, and all the paperwork was signed, I felt very sad that we hadn't known more about hospice earlier. It could have helped tremendously in the last stages of both the girls' lives. The program helps the family by delivering all medications and supplies to the home, having nurses and therapists on call and counseling, but most of all being the advocate and coordinator between the insurance company and the patient. That is priceless. Over the past few years, the countless amount of time and energy I had spent on the phone trying to coordinate all the care and then trying to get the insurance company to pay the bills could have been time spent with the girls. If only I had known.

༄༅

Jeff flew to California on Monday. Darius stayed home from work and spent the day with Vanessa, cuddled with her in their room. Vanessa made a list of people she asked me to call so she could say good-bye. Stephanie, her best friend, came by several times a day. She had just started a job right up the street so she would be able to visit more often. She had always been there for Vanessa and continued to be there now.

Sebastiani, her feral cat, appeared on Tuesday, sitting on the deck looking through the sliding glass doors. She stayed in the same place for three days. Friends and family came and went. The nights were scary for all of us. Vanessa was having frequent episodes of not being able to breathe and panicking to get air. Jeff and I stayed at the apartment all the time now, sprawled at night on a futon on the living room floor; not that we slept. We needed to be there to help Darius when she had these crises.

All through the night the alarm on the Pulsox machine kept going off. The machine measured her oxygen levels, and it sounded if the numbers were dropping too low. After two nights, we turned off the alarm; her numbers were so low now the alarm never stopped. Instead, we placed the machine in the bedroom doorway facing us so at anytime during the night we could look up and see the red numbers flashing. I didn't sleep a wink watching.

The constant rhythm of the bi-pap machine filled the air, adding to the noise of the fan, her air purifier and the whoosh of air from her oxygen tank. It was the background noise she had grown used to and couldn't sleep without. Like Charlotte, she didn't want to hear herself breathing.

Our friend Betsy happened to be in southern California, so she flew up on Tuesday to visit Vanessa, not knowing until she came how bad things really were. She brought light and laughter to us that day.

I don't know where Vanessa found the strength, but she spoke on the phone to a few of her longtime friends. She also said good-bye to her Nan in Pennsylvania. Months before she had written in her journal what pieces of jewelry and special things she wanted given to friends and family.

On Tuesday, she took off the necklace she was wearing and put it on me as I sat next to her on the bed. She loved her "treasures" and wanted to make sure that everyone would remember her through them. By evening, she was very weak and we didn't think she would make it through the night.

Wednesday morning when she opened her big brown eyes, the first thing she said was "I am sorry. I woke up. I said good-bye to so many people yesterday and I didn't die." I couldn't help but laugh and cry at the same time; it was such a Vanessa statement.

ॐ

As we had with Charlotte, we each spent time alone with Vanessa. "I am so lucky to be your mom," I told her. "It will always be the most important thing I will ever do in my life, I'm so proud of you, of your strength and your caring. I don't know what I am going to do without you in my world. You will always be in my heart; wherever I go, you will be with me." We sat holding hands and she looked at me, the lower half of her face hidden in the now ever present bi-pap mask. She spoke slowly through the din of the machines in her room. "Mom, I have the easy part, I just have to die, but you, dad and Darius will be left behind, that's the hard part."

On Wednesday night around eleven o'clock we were all in the bedroom. Vanessa was propped up on some pillows when she suddenly sat up and said, "I've had enough," and pulled the bi-pap mask off her face. She looked at us and said, "I knew the bi-pap was hard on my lungs, but.." and she never finished the sentence. She slowly fell back onto the pillow as she lost consciousness. It was the same time of night that Charlotte had slipped into a coma only four months before.

Darius lay down next to her on one side of the bed and I on the other, speaking to her as I had for Charlotte. Soon Darius fell asleep holding her hand. Jeff stood vigil next to the bed. She was very restless even as I gave her small amounts of morphine through her stomach tube. She just didn't settle.

Several times she would open her eyes and look at me as if through a mist, reaching out her arms to touch me, then falling back onto the pillows. At two thirty, I called hospice and asked them what to do because she seemed as if she wanted to get up, but she was not conscious. They said we should go to the hospital and pick up an order for Ativan, an anti-anxiety drug. Jeff went over and picked it up, crushed the tablet into some water and we squirted it into her stomach tube. By four, she quieted.

I continued stroking her hair and talking to her about life on the farm when suddenly I could feel Charlotte in the room, coming to be by Vanessa's side to help her sister through the journey.

And she did, because Vanessa didn't seem to drown in mucus as Charlotte had or take one deep breath at the end. Instead, she silently, peacefully faded away, her breath becoming more and more shallow, fainter and fainter, until there was no more. I had my hand on her heart and could feel the beats getting weaker and weaker, not wanting to stop and then they did, as softly as a whisper.

Charlotte and Vanessa both died on a Thursday, only one hour apart in time, time marked silently every day now.

Chapter 50

Vanessa, Darius

"It is hard dying, but it is harder leaving the ones you love and having to say goodbye. I hate the fact that I have to leave and feel so bad that I have to go."

Vanessa

We each had time alone with Vanessa as Jeff began calling people back east. Sebastiani was no longer holding vigil on the porch; she left when Vanessa died. Soon, the house was filled with family and friends.

As I washed Vanessa's body, I couldn't help but think about Charlotte. She had looked so stressed after she died, probably from having the bi-pap on all night. It was too much; it took longer for her to die than necessary. Vanessa on the other hand looked almost angelic and everyone who came into the room said the same thing. She looked completely at peace, better than she had looked in weeks, as if she was ready to say something, never having left us at all.

The amazing thing was that Charlotte had been ready in many ways; she was tired; her body had been in pain for a long time. Vanessa was the opposite. She was not ready and said that right up to the end. She still wanted to go to Hawaii, and told us that her body felt strong, she still had more fight, but her lungs did not. So why did she look so at peace? I think it was because Charlotte was with her.

Charlotte had always said she wanted to be the first to go and maybe that was why, so she could be there to help her sister when she passed. I felt her there with us and the evidence was the look on Vanessa's face, peaceful and not afraid. The funny thing is anyone who knew them would have guessed that Charlotte would have been the one to look angelic and at peace, not Vanessa, but the opposite was true.

Braiding her hair for the last time took me back to when they were young. Brushing and braiding their hair was always a part of our daily routine; French braids were their favorite and also mine. Even as they grew older, especially in the hospital, they still asked if I would brush and braid their hair; it was an intimate and special time together. Vanessa could sit for hours, saying she thought she liked it because it reminded her of having her head touched in the isolette when we were not yet able to hold her. Her hair now was super fine, waist long and easily tangled, so it could take a long time to get all the knots out; that part she did not enjoy and she let you know it.

&

Late in the afternoon when it was time to call the funeral home, I went into the bedroom and cut Vanessa's braid, the one I had woven only hours before. The day before, she had asked me to cut her hair and donate it for cancer patients. I promised her I would.

I removed each of the rings from Vanessa's fingers, rings she wore every day. Her engagement ring from Darius, her antique blue sapphire ring from childhood, her sapphire band from Aunt Janice, and several tiny gold bands. The last piece of jewelry I removed was her beloved gold charm bracelet, her life captured upon her wrist, each charm with its own story. She jingled wherever she went and had been collecting charms ever since she was eleven years old. It had come off only when she wanted to add another charm. The bracelet was now full; there was no room left for any more stories.

She had asked a few days before if it was okay if Darius kept it after she died. I agreed; he was the one to continue their story.

Vanessa always had her little treasures around, especially her old stuffed teddy bear Ted, and Ellie, her tattered, stuffed yellow elephant, keeping her memories of childhood close at hand. They seemed to prove she had lived, loved and been a part of life, not to be forgotten.

When the people from the funeral home arrived to take Vanessa, we wrapped her in the quilt she had received from Lois and draped her with the same blue velvet cloth that had covered Charlotte only four months before. We placed several of her engagement flowers and Ted into her arms.

She was slowly carried through the living room, out to the landing and down the steep wooden steps. At the bottom of the stairs, they carried her past Darius' car, which was parked in the driveway. Vanessa loved that Audi station wagon and the sense of freedom it gave her. She always sat in the front passenger seat, ready for any foray into the outside world, especially during the last few months of her life. As her stamina waned, Darius would fill up an oxygen tank or two and take her for a ride, sometimes so she could watch him surf, sometimes just on an errand; it was something she always looked forward to.

As they carried Vanessa's body past the passenger door, the car alarm went off. Startled, we looked at one another and said in unison, "Oh, my God, it's the girls." I don't why but we all felt they were playing a joke on us, and laughing. Jeff, who was standing at the bottom of the steps, confirmed they hadn't touched the car. We asked Darius if the car alarm had ever gone off before and he said, "No, it's the first time it ever happened. I didn't even know it had an alarm."

It was so appropriate. All I knew was that we all felt the same thing, at the same time, and couldn't explain why it made us smile, even laugh, as if we could see the girls being playful with us. It would have been just like them.

Chapter 51

Vanessa

I go from thee! God only knows
How I have longed to stay—
How I have shuddered thus to tread,
The lone and shadowed way.
Faith tells me that I soon may know
The joys the blessed find,
And yet I falter while I cast
A lingering look behind.

Sent from Emily Mannheimer

A few days later, I found Thomas' Travels, the children's book Vanessa was working on. It was almost finished; only six pages remained to be illustrated.

I brought it to my sister's house along with Vanessa's colored pencils, and started drawing. It was as if her hand was guiding mine through the unfinished pages. When I finally placed the pencils back into the box and put all the finished pages in order, I realized I had worked straight through for several days. It felt so good to forget everything and concentrate on something so close to Vanessa. When I saw Darius, I asked him to look at the book and he wasn't able to tell where Vanessa had stopped and I had continued. It was what I had hoped for; her hand had become a part of mine.

ⅆⅆ

When Vanessa died, Rusty, from the Philadelphia Inquirer, called me in California to say he would write Vanessa's obituary, as he had for Charlotte. We spent a lot of time on the details and I express mailed some pictures to him. As he did for Charlotte, he captured Vanessa's essence in the article. It appeared on Tuesday, March 28th.

That evening, Rusty called to say that the editor of the paper saw the obituary and wanted to do a feature article about the girls for the Sunday edition. There were many phone calls and lots of pictures passing back and forth across the country that week as we pieced together their story.

I was still in California on Sunday and couldn't buy the Philadelphia paper so I cranked up the computer and looked on line. When I opened the site, I couldn't believe my eyes. There the lead headline at the top of the page read, "To prepare for this pain, 25 years was not enough." Next to the headline was a picture of Charlotte and Vanessa taken when they were students in California. What instantly flashed in my mind was that the girls were laughing, happy to know they were front-page news.

It was ironic that they always wanted to be famous and famous they were, but under very different circumstances than they would have imagined, than anyone would have imagined. Because this was the lead story in the Sunday paper, it was picked up by United Press International and distributed throughout the United States. For months, we received letters and phone calls from people all over the country saying how deeply touched they were by the girls' story.

ⅆⅆ

Amidst all of this, I also had to plan for Vanessa's memorials. We chose the same shaped urn as Charlotte's, only this time we glazed the background a cream color, instead of mint; similar, but not the same, again the twin connection. Encircling the lid, Jeff painted Vanessa's gold charm bracelet with some of her favorite charms. Darius painted an elephant,

234

her favorite animal. As his mom sat watching she asked, "Darius why is your hand shaking, why are you so nervous?" "I am under a lot of pressure. Whenever I do anything for Vanessa, whether it's buying a present or shopping for food, I want to do it right." It made me smile to see he still wanted to please her.

❧

With a sense of humor like her dad's, I am sure Vanessa would have approved the date of her memorial, Saturday, April 1, 2000, April Fools Day. It was held in a mission-style church, now a national landmark, that sits high on a hill in Tiburon, overlooking San Francisco Bay. Gracing the long wooden pews were wildflowers from the surrounding hills, stitched into the needlepoint cushions made by the ladies who cared for the historical site. The setting was simple and elegant, much like Vanessa.

Chris Davis officiated the service as he had for Charlotte. He again shared his experiences, only this time he focused on Vanessa. "Pat and Jeff's philosophy and tradition of letting the girls experience life were tested when Vanessa and Charlotte wanted and did move to California. Vanessa simply said to me, 'they let us come. They knew how happy we were out here.'

"Vanessa said something similar to me once in regard to people who visit her. 'There are those who pop in and out, not committing to any kind of serious relationship. They are there for a moment and then they go off into their own lives without glancing back. There are people who visit and have their own agendas. They never see me because they are so caught up in themselves. And then there are people willing to just be there.'

"Early on in life, Vanessa began to understand through her art, that each moment in life was a gift and if we chose to see it that way, we could begin to seize the unlimited amount of opportunities life provides and use them in order to give and receive happiness.

"A little over nine years ago she met and fell in love with Darius. As their relationship grew and their love for each other deepened, Vanessa discovered new sources and new motivations for expressing her art and for sharing the gift of life with others. Vanessa's life wisdom rose out of her deep understanding of who she was as Vanessa Robbins. She was not only a daughter, or only a twin, or only a person with cystic fibrosis. Yes, all these things made up parts of who Vanessa was, but they did not define her as a person. She was given this life, knowing practically from the beginning what the final scene would be, and yet she still chose to play the part, to live her life the way she did. Now the stage is empty."

As the service ended, the bell rang several times in the old bell tower and echoed within the walls of the church. We were later told it hadn't been rung in many years due to its fragile state, but today the staff of the church wanted to pay tribute to Vanessa. This was their gift to her.

Jeff and I walked out into the brilliant California sunshine and silently took in the magnificent view of San Francisco Bay. Dr. Margolin walked over to us a few minutes later and said, "Of all the patients I've ever known, Vanessa was the most together person I have ever met. She understood her condition so well and knew what she was up against, yet she kept on fighting and always had a smile for us no matter how bad she felt. I will miss her."

Chapter 52

Vanessa

"The time has come to say good-bye, a time to remember, a time to cry."

Vanessa

We returned to Pennsylvania for the final memorial. The night before the service, we gathered in our living room to place the remainder of Vanessa's ashes into the urn. Darius had kept some in California to be spread where Vanessa used to sit and watch him surf, and later on a beach in Hawaii. The rest he brought in the elephant piggy bank I had as a little girl, which Vanessa had a long time ago added to her collection. These ashes Jeff and I later spread on the beach in Ocean City, New Jersey, where the girls used to play in the summer, at Betsy and Michael's house in Chester Springs where they celebrated their 21st birthday, and at Ray and Pat's house, where Charlotte was married and both girls had many happy memories. The remainder we still have in the elephant piggy bank next to Vanessa's picture.

Before we poured the other half into her urn, we laid the other butterfly magnet from Christine, only a different color than the one for Charlotte. Then on top of the ashes, we placed the dried rose petals from my garden that I had saved when Charlotte died. Darius brought sand from their favorite California beach and flowers from the hillside. I placed wild rosemary from the hills surrounding their apartment where I sometimes walked when Vanessa was taking a nap. On top we laid purple and yellow pansies from Charlotte's grave. "There's rosemary, that's for remembrance; pray, love, remember. And there is pansies, that's for thoughts." Ophelia's line from Hamlet, a role Vanessa had played in high school.

✌✍

I hope Vanessa was present on April 26, 2000 as the church filled to capacity and then trailed out the door; it would have brought a smile to her face. But I am sure both Charlotte and Vanessa were there, together.

The day was cool and cloudy, the opposite of Charlotte's sunny, seventy-degree day in December. Pastor Dan officiated the service and wrote a tribute capturing Vanessa's spirit.

> *"She was dealt a tough hand in life. Most of her life she lived with a persistent, greedy, debilitating physical condition. It would have been easy to understand how a person, living under such circumstances, could become cynical and self-absorbed. Vanessa chose the higher road. She chose love as her guiding light. She did not endure life. She lived life; a life that radiated love. Just look around this sanctuary. What power other than love could fill this place in tribute to one so young.*
>
> *"Vanessa's love did not gently float in on gossamer wings. No, Vanessa's love was served up on a plain platter of truth and honesty. She knew her time with us would be limited. Therefore, she was focused and deliberate in everything she did. She was not long suffering of empty talk.*
>
> *"Vanessa knew exactly who she was physically, emotionally and spiritually. This self-knowledge, along with her open honesty and nurturing spirit were key ingredients in a personality that attracted so many people."*

In the memorial tribute program, Darius wrote:

> *"Vanessa, you made me feel special. The love you gave to me was truly inspiring. I am a better man for each day we had together. Someone as*

special as you, never truly dies. Thank you for being the gift you were.
I love you, Vanessa."

⚥⚥

The church overflowed with people from our past and present lives, old friends, the girls' high school teachers, their third grade teacher, even their sixth grade gym teacher. He said he still had their picture on his bulletin board and told new students about them and how hard the girls had worked to keep up with all the other kids. They never used their illness as an excuse.

Rich, the woodworker from Playschool, told a story about the girls at summer camp.

> "Early one morning, Charlotte and Vanessa walked over to the woodworking shop and asked if they could build a house. Now, during the six weeks of camp, I build small toy boats and such with the kids, not a house, but I thought I would keep them interested. 'Well let's see, I need to speak to Miss Betty because I don't have enough wood to build a house.' They said, 'that's okay, we'll go and ask Miss Betty and come back tomorrow to let you know what she said.'
>
> "The next morning when I came in, outside the workshop was a large stack of wood, enough to build a playhouse. Charlotte and Vanessa came by first thing, happy to see the wood and wanting to start right away. I asked them to take a seat so we could discuss the project. 'What type of house do you want to build?' "Big," was their reply in unison and all I could do was laugh.
>
> "Needless to say, we worked together and built the house over the next six weeks and it actually survived for many years. When they no longer attended camp, it was passed on to the next group of campers with the story of how it was built. What I loved about them was that they believed anything was possible."

As he spoke about the girls, I couldn't help but smile; nothing was too big an obstacle for the girls to overcome and their determination and enthusiasm usually won out.

My friend Kathy Spencer and her husband John were there with their new baby girl Caroline, born on the day Vanessa died, March 23rd, after 44 hours of labor and by caesarian section, almost the same way Vanessa came into this world.

Jeff spoke about Vanessa's love of writing poetry. He recalled a story from when she was in high school. "Vanessa had written one of her many poems for an English class assignment and when it came back from her teacher, it was mentioned that she thought it would be a better poem if it didn't rhyme. Vanessa, true to form, wrote back some two pages about why it needed to rhyme and would keep it the way she had written it. It was her poem and it wasn't changing."

Later in the service, Michael Bacon performed "Let Me Memorize You," a song he had written and a favorite of Vanessa's, one she had requested for the service. Before beginning, he said, "Vanessa wanted me to sing this song for her and luckily for me, it rhymes."

❧❦

Jeff and I are so grateful for all the stories that were shared with us that day. Vanessa and Charlotte were remembered as pure at heart, honest and witty young women, who struggled for so long to keep their identity and spirit from disappearing in bodies that were constantly sending them one more challenge to conquer. They achieved it for as long as they could.

❧❦

After the service, a long line of friends and family again stretched across the road, from the church to the graveside, only this time Darius, not Caleb, led the way.

Kneeling down when we reached the grave, I placed the urn Darius handed to me into the center of the small open grave next to Charlotte's. On either side of the urn, I placed their threadbare, much loved Snoopy pillows, carried everywhere when they were young. Over it all, I scattered rose petals. But this time there was more.

Vanessa loved Fig Newtons and the night before, I saw half a packet open in the closet, leftover from when she was home for Charlotte's memorial. Removing them from the cellophane wrapper, I dropped them in; one at a time, hoping she might like them for her journey.

We gathered once again at Pat's house after the service. I don't remember much except that several people came up and told me that during the entire graveside service, adjacent to the cemetery on the farm, two white horses stood watching from the split rail fence. When the service ended, as if released, they both reared up and with tails held high in the air, ran all the way across the field to the top of the hill where they turned and for the longest time looked back at the cemetery.

🙢🙠

Several days later, we received a letter from a family Vanessa had babysat for during high school. Charlotte and Vanessa started babysitting when they were twelve years old and continued until they went away to college, sought after every weekend. The kids looked forward to their visits because the girls always had something planned for them to do, from making goodies to putting on a play and video-taping the kids in the process. The parents loved the girls' enthusiasm and the fun they all had. When they were in high school, they spent a few summers as mother's helpers. The letter I received was from one of these mothers.

> *Dear Pat, Jeff and Joyce,* [Joyce is my mother]
> *I was so saddened to hear about both Charlotte and Vanessa this week. Although they will always be your angels, they were angels to us years ago. I truly believe that God was watching out for our family the summer I hired Vanessa to be our "mother's helper." Only God knew that Aaron would have that terrible brain injury and that I would spend weeks with him in the hospital. Vanessa brought us hope and strength that only someone who had been through so many hospital procedures herself could. She gave Aaron confidence in the medical profession; she helped him see himself as handsome although he had his head shaved; and she was there for him to talk to when he was still very scared.*
> *Besides that she played with the other children, fed them, changed diapers, answered the phone and did anything we asked without complaint. As a matter of fact she brought the excitement of teenage life into our house. She talked endlessly about Darius, and so*

hopefully of her acting career. Two of my children are now acting in high school plays. Aaron has had lead parts in the Malvern Prep spring and fall plays since ninth grade. It will not surprise me if he decides on an acting career himself. Kristen started this year in ninth grade in the chorus of 42nd Street. I feel that Vanessa's love for acting encouraged both of them to participate.

Although many teenagers have difficulty with their parents, and I am sure you had your moments, both of your girls displayed deep love and respect for you and their grandmother. I can only hope that we can have the same feelings with our children.

I hope that you can find peace and hope by knowing that your children touched our lives so profoundly that pieces of them do live on in my children. They were and always will be our angels.

With deepest love and sympathy,
Kathy

Chapter 53

Pat, Charlotte

"Sometimes the pain of missing them rushes over me in a suffocating sadness, as if a blanket has been thrown over me, leaving me in total isolation. I need to feel this. I will never accomplish anything in life more important than being Charlotte and Vanessa's mom."

Pat

My life as I knew it had ended, and a second, entirely new one began, whether I wanted to be a part of it or not. Days blurred into weeks and then into months, and then into years.

I left my job at the end of June, three months after Vanessa died. It required too much physical and emotional energy to keep up the front needed to hide my overwhelming grief. I didn't want to hold it at bay anymore, needing to open up the wound and let it bleed, let myself be sad whenever I wanted and go through the journey. It had been too long a struggle, never having a chance to grieve after Charlotte died and now the reason to be strong was also gone; I was tired.

When they say, "filled with grief", I understood those words now. Charlotte and Vanessa were my life, my reason for living. I had to take the time to feel what life was like without them in this world and learn how to cope with it.

When I ventured out, people were still moving forward in their lives and there I was standing still, asking, "Don't you know they are gone, how can life keep moving forward?" I now understood why everyone asks that question when you are grieving. It is the beginning of the process.

I still performed the basic functions of life, just without caring or feeling. The days went by very slowly and I marked time.

For a few weeks, after a fitful sleep I would wake up every day at 5:45 am and relive the moments before they died and wonder what I could have done differently. After a while, it was only a few days a week and then just every Thursday morning. What could I have done to ease their way?

Weeks went by and as time passed, I gratefully started to feel the girls, sometimes in good ways and sometimes in funny ways. These connections seemed like coincidences, but when they happened I knew they were more than that and I wholeheartedly opened up to them.

For all the years the girls were in my life, they were the focus of my days, my work, my play and joy in this world. Jeff and I concentrated our energy on creating a lifestyle to keep them as healthy and happy as possible. Our world revolved around them, and taking care of them was our purpose. Now, it was as if the roles had been reversed.

Now, Charlotte and Vanessa started taking care of us, just as we once took care of them, by sending us little signs that they were helping us in our journey here without them. And I must say they were busy from the start.

Weeks after Vanessa's memorial, the mountain pinks burst into bloom across the cemetery; it was time to remove the wreaths and plant something new. My mom and I went to the garden store and carefully picked out two vibrant pink verbena plants and planted them on their graves.

By the end of the week, Charlotte's had lots of bright pink blossoms with new buds popping out all over, Vanessa's was another story. All of the original buds had dropped off and within two weeks the plant had withered and turned brown, despite all the watering and encouragement. Not one bud had bloomed.

We went back to the store, bought another healthy pink verbena with lots of buds, pulled out the old plant and put in the new, even surrounding it with rich new soil. Again, the same thing happened, not one of the buds bloomed. No amount of water or nurturing helped, it shriveled up and died two weeks later.

I talked to my sister, who has a green thumb, about the mystery, and we realized that pink was not Vanessa's favorite color. More important, it was the same color as Charlotte's plant; again, the twin thing. What was I thinking?

My mom and I pulled out the latest withered plant and this time planted a purple verbena, the same plant only a different color. After several days, the buds burst into bloom and both the pink and purple plant thrived all summer.

So, I learned my lesson, no pink flowers on Vanessa's grave. She made that clear, but most important, she was still having her say.

∅⊱

The summer came and once again, I picked raspberries for Charlotte and Vanessa. On the border of the woods, near the cemetery and the farm they grew up on, there are wild raspberry bushes. It was the end of June and the sun was setting, spreading a rosy hue over the entire hillside. I walked along the edge of the woods and picked some nice, fat, juicy raspberries and popped them into my mouth.

I could taste the sunshine as they burst open on my tongue. At that moment, a soft warm breeze glanced across my face and I said hello to the girls. After I had eaten my fill, I carefully picked some especially big ones, filling two small glasses to the brim and walked up the hill to place a glass on each of the girls' graves, hoping they would like my offering.

∅⊱

The girls continued to work their magic through Mother Nature and mostly through flowers. Mama cactus flowered for the first time that year on Thursday, May eleventh, six months after Charlotte died. For Charlotte's one-year memorial, I bought a white orchid with the subtlest hint of pink. It had a single stem, which halfway up the plant, split into two, each with many delicate buds. As soon as I saw it, I thought of the girls, together, yet separate. The garden center said that the flowers would last about six weeks. The orchid continued to bloom for over five months and was still in bloom for Vanessa's first memorial, March 23.

Darius' mom called on the one-year anniversary of Vanessa's death and told me that the orchid we had given her from Vanessa's room had bloomed that day. For years to come, it continued blooming, including the sixth year when it put forth six flowers on the day of her anniversary.

⬦⬦

The connections continued. In April, Charlotte's best friend, Brooke, called to say she was pregnant with her second child. "Are you sitting down? I am due to deliver on December 3, Charlotte's birthday. If it's a girl, we are going to name her Charlotte. How could we not, when all the signs pointed to Charlotte having something to do with this." I couldn't agree with her more.

On November 11th, Charlotte's first memorial, Brooke started contractions, which persisted throughout the day. She thought she was in labor and said out loud to Charlotte, "I need more time," and by that evening the contractions subsided. On December first, Brooke called. "Congratulations, you are grandparents and you're not going to believe it, but everyone in the room was so amazed when Charlotte was born, because she actually came out smiling." I was sure Charlotte was smiling too.

⬦⬦

In autumn, I couldn't help but send Stephanie, Vanessa's best friend in California, a priority mail envelope filled with the most colorful leaves Jeff and I could find. We started sending these packages to Charlotte and Vanessa when they went away to college and continued through the years. They said it reminded them of the sights and smells of our years on the farm, and Stephanie, a nature lover, was happy that the tradition lived on.

⬦⬦

My life revolved around the next date associated with the girls. August sixteenth, Charlotte's second wedding anniversary. November eleventh, the first anniversary of Charlotte's death. December third, Vanessa and Charlotte's twenty-sixth birthday. Our first Thanksgiving and

Christmas without the girls. By the end of January, I was anticipating the first anniversary of Vanessa's death in March and then it too passed. I had spent the entire year anticipating the next mark in time on the calendar, absolutely numb in my body and soul, struggling for some semblance of living.

ॐ

The winter had been a very long one; I worked hard at grieving, it was all I knew. I didn't see many of my friends during the year. I was alone most of the week since Jeff traveled almost every week to Chattanooga, leaving on Monday and returning on Friday.

But being alone enabled me to go to the depths of my sorrow, to work on how I would now live in this world, to cry as much as I wanted for as long as I wanted with no one to hurt or question me. Many times when I was struggling, I didn't want to confide in Jeff because he was doing okay at that moment and I didn't want to throw him quickly into the same state I was in. He needed respite too, but it put a tremendous strain on our relationship. I do understand why there is such a high divorce rate after the death of a child; the connection between you is so fragile at this time and there is no passion in your life to drown in.

ॐ

In April, the following year, I was invited to spend some time with friends in Houston. We had only gotten together with them once in the past ten years. The girls babysat for their kids before they moved to Houston and over the years we really hadn't had much connection, except updates in Christmas cards.

Although reticent to go, I decided it might be a good change for me. Since the girls had died, Jenny and I kept in touch by email and during that time her husband, Jeff, had been diagnosed and was doing battle with kidney cancer.

I had never been to Houston, and it seemed like a good time to visit.

As the day drew near to leave, I became nervous about spending a full week with Jenny and her husband. My body and mind were just starting to recover and it still took a lot of effort to be around people.

I kept asking myself if I was ready to get back on a plane, heading into unknown territory, but in the end, I decided to go. I needed to go.

At the airport as I was waiting to board, a woman came and sat next to me. Looking nervous she told me this was the first time she had ever flown, which surprised me, as she did not look young. "Don't worry, it's a big plane and the weather looks fine," was all I could muster.

The flight was smooth as predicted until we were twenty minutes from landing. Then the intercom clicked on. "This is the pilot speaking. Houston airport has just been closed due to severe thunderstorms, heavy rains and hail. We'll try to stay away from the turbulence as much as possible, but keep your seat belts fastened. I'll get back to you in twenty minutes; the good news is the weather generally passes through Houston quickly." Thirty minutes later, he was back on. "Houston airport is still closed and we are getting low on fuel. We are trying to get clearance to land in either Waco, Texas, or New Orleans. We are checking for available gates so I'll let you know."

We rode out the storm trapped in the clouds, dropping swiftly and then riding quickly back up on other currents. I couldn't help thinking of the woman I had spoken to earlier and wondered what must be going through her mind, most likely, "I will never fly again."

When I left home this time, I had made sure Jeff knew to whom I wanted all of my possessions to go in case of emergency and that conversation quickly passed through my mind, but it felt okay. Peering out the window, I saw that we were moving through massive thunderstorm clouds, some dark and ominous, others white with streaks of sunlight breaking through. I felt we were on the Titanic watching icebergs float by, waiting for one to hit.

After we circled another thirty minutes, there was another click. "We have been cleared to land in New Orleans and have been assigned a gate, although I am sorry to say, folks, that as of this moment, there is no flight crew available for the trip to Houston."

Some loud groans were uttered; I groaned too, knowing we had a long wait ahead. But less than a minute later, the pilot was back. "The plan has changed; we are going in to Houston airport. Please prepare for an immediate landing." I couldn't help thinking that we really were in Texas where the pilots were cowboys at heart. We dropped quickly in altitude and then came in for a low, long, and bumpy ride down, but we landed safely and in Houston.

My fears about coming were allayed right from the start when Jenny met me at the airport. We were very comfortable with each other and this grew as the week went by. We did the usual sight seeing and had dinners, with many laughs and some tears, but for me it was much more than that.

One night at dinner we were laughing at something when her husband Jeff said, "It's so good to see you laugh again. The girls would be so happy. They would want you to laugh. It's okay." All of a sudden I felt a release. I needed permission from someone who had not been through the pain of the last few years; someone who because of distance could see more clearly, someone who was actually engaged in life.

That week, we all connected in a way I was ready for, needing to be a part of life again. The trip was a turning point for me.

Chapter 54

65 Roses Cover

65 Roses

Written and Illustrated by
Charlotte and Vanessa Robbins

"All of these are memories of lives I have touched and joys I have shared."

A week after I returned from Houston, a letter came in the mail. Not able to take my eyes off the words in front of me, I dropped into a chair as I read the following:

Dear Pat:

This is going to be a strange letter, and I'm nervous writing this to you. I know that we don't really know each other, and the last thing I want to do is to upset someone (nor—to be honest—to look like an idiot). But I also know that if I don't pass this on for you to do with as you will, I'll always feel guilty wondering if I made a mistake by being afraid. So please disregard this entirely if you wish. I just ask you to trust that I am sending it with the very best of intentions. I will just tell you what happened, and let you follow your gut instinct about it:

Last Thursday night, April 26th, I dreamed this same dream four times. I woke up three times, got up, then went back to sleep, and each time I dreamed this same dream, exact in every detail. This is something that rarely happens to me, and another reason I think it may be important.

In the dream, I was being told something by unseen beings. Because there was a completely natural, familiar, good, innocent feel or sense to the communication, I took these beings to be my guides or messengers from the Light. I did not see them—they seemed to be communicating in spirit form without presenting a physical appearance.

I understood them to say that I knew a woman named Pat Robinson who has two grown daughters on the other side. I immediately denied this, saying that the only person I could think of by that name was the man who runs that religious television station (I was thinking of Pat Robertson and mixing up the name). They said no, no, that this is a woman I know or know of from work.

I thought a moment and then told them that there used to be a Pat Robinson who managed the Development office, and they said "not quite, but you're thinking of the right person." (I take that to mean that I was still mixing up the name.)

I said I knew she had lost a daughter not too long ago. They said yes, that was the right person, but they insisted "she has two daughters here." I argued politely and said I thought it was only one, but they said again, "No, it is two." They then said, "Mother's Day is coming soon and her daughters want to send her a huge bouquet of red roses and tell her they are happy and well, and that she was the best mother they could ever have wanted and that they just want her to know this."

As I said, I never saw anyone physical or communicated directly with this daughter or daughters, so I have nothing logical to back up the strong sense I got of a very vibrant, enthusiastic, laughing young woman that—for some reason I have no logic for at all—I took to be blonde. What struck me most, though, was the sense of real excitement and joy that seemed to be coming from this girl and from the guides who were speaking to me.

I asked why they were telling me this when I didn't know Pat personally and that she would probably think I was crazy if I told her this. They said it was because 1) they were able to get through to me clearly (I don't think it is me. It's them; they were very determined—

they sent the same dream message four times in succession! That's hard to ignore.) 2) Because I know who they are talking about and 3) because they know I will believe the message is real and trust that they are sincere. (I do pay attention to dreams, and believe that sometimes there are messages, sometimes it's just the subconscious working through our conscious life. But in the past when I've gotten messages, they've been for or about me, not others). I'm pretty skeptical—in spite of how it might seem—and so I answered that just because I might believe the message was real didn't mean Pat would. The main reason I believe it is real is because I know this did not come from my subconscious; there is no way.

They asked me to try to deliver the message. I said that I didn't think Pat worked at the hospital any more, and so didn't know if it was possible, but that I would try, and what did they want me to say. They then repeated that the daughter(s) were just sending their love via a gigantic bouquet of strikingly beautiful, fragrant roses. (I saw the roses, but not the daughter(s) or the speakers, and it truly was a gigantic, perfectly amazing bouquet of long-stemmed red roses—so huge that it would take both arms to hold them all—much bigger than I've seen beauty contestants on TV carrying. And they said there was an equally huge wish coming to Pat for a very happy Mother's Day. They said they just want Pat to know that they are around her and loving her and interested in her life, just like they always were.

I asked why this particular Mother's Day, what was special about it compared to every other one, and they very gently told me it was none of my business. They didn't use those words, of course; they said, "There is a reason, but if you could just pass on the message, her daughters would appreciate it so much." I said again that I thought there was just one daughter, and they said (patiently and kindly) could I please just deliver the message as I was receiving it?

I said I'd meditate on it and would try to do that if it seemed the right thing to do. They said thank you, and that was the end, except that it was repeated four times in identical fashion.

Without explaining any of this to anyone at all (and I will not, this is private), I asked Norma Hall if she would add your address to a stamped envelope and mail it on to you. She said yes. I did not ask for your address (and she wouldn't have given it if I had). I am hoping *you do not find this message intrusive. I just didn't know quite what else to do.*

    Pat Walton

It took me a few minutes to regain my composure, and while smiling and crying at the same time, I gratefully felt my body relax for the first time in a very long time. Charlotte and Vanessa were okay.

I read the letter over and over again and a deep sigh of relief washed over me. Yes, they were okay. Since they had died, all I kept asking for was the knowledge that they were okay and this letter answered that for me. It didn't make me miss them any less, it just took away the fear that they were still struggling somewhere.

A few weeks before, I had bought a small handmade card with a long stemmed red rose painted on it because it reminded me of the girls, thinking I would send it to a friend. It was lying in front of me on the dining room table so I sent it to Pat Walton, thanking her for writing such a difficult letter and asking if she could meet with me sometime. I included my phone number. She called as soon as she received the card.

We met at the hospital coffee shop and since we had printed several of the children's books the girls' had created, I brought a copy of *65 Roses* to show her the connection to the dream. As she read the words, tears came to her eyes.

She explained how the excitement and enthusiasm she felt in all four dreams was so strong and full of determination that she had to act on it. "I felt it didn't matter what happened, I had to let you know. I didn't feel like I had a choice."

"You know Pat," I told her, "when I read the letter, so many things connected for me. You dreamt this on a Thursday, they both died on a Thursday; the roses; Mothers Day; letting me know they were okay, and especially the feeling of excitement emanating from them. How much like the girls to be so creative and connect through a stranger so I would believe the message. I love it."

The following Sunday was Mother's Day. Jeff and I placed long stem red roses on their graves, in honor of their message. I actually could smile and thank them for making this Mother's Day so special. I felt like a mom again. I felt they were there with me just as they had said in the dream.

Chapter 55

Pat, Jeff

"If I could give some words of advice, I would say take time in life to take a deep breath and look at what's around you and what makes you happy and the people who are important to you and then take the time to tell them that. Tell them you love them and let them know how you feel. It's not going to hurt any situation; it's only going to make your relationship stronger."

Vanessa

Jeff and I traveled back to Houston at the end of May for our friend Jeff's surprise fiftieth birthday party. We spent the first few days in San Antonio for my fiftieth, and then traveled up to Houston. It was a hard trip for both of us, but for some reason I could feel the girls all around me that weekend.

On the plane trip home, sitting next to one other, we were miles apart. I was thinking how upset the girls would be if Jeff and I didn't make it, if we separated, as the majority of couples do under these circumstances. I wanted to reconnect again, physically and emotionally, and not lose the most important person in my life, but I didn't know how. It seemed like such an effort when I didn't feel passion for anything.

Jeff had never been a talker and now the circumstances of our life only made him withdraw more, but I couldn't hold it in any longer. "I don't know if I can go on in my life feeling so sad," I said. "Will we ever be able to feel joy again, feel alive again? Will we ever actually feel passion again? I'm scared, Jeff. The girls would be so upset if we don't make it, but I don't know if I can keep going on this way."

He turned to me and told me things I had never known before, things he had locked away, like his feelings of insecurity in our relationship, thinking I would leave him one day. And now he felt that day was coming because we were so distant and detached. I guess I needed to hear his fears, his vulnerability and his openness because something snapped in me as he spoke. I don't know what or how or why, but from one instant to the next, something wonderful happened; I felt a spark of life, a twinge of passion flow into my body, bringing it back to life. It happened that suddenly and it still amazes me how fast my thoughts influenced my body, changing the direction of our life in a moment. I will never be able to explain it and I am sure the girls had their hand in it; they were planning their magical surprise all weekend.

On the ride home in the car, all we wanted to do was kiss, the long deep kisses of long ago. It was so exciting to feel my body come alive again. It was funny because a few weeks later, a neighbor mentioned that lately he noticed when Jeff would go to work in the morning, we looked like newlyweds at the door saying good-bye. Yes, it definitely was the girls' doing.

ॐ

I started finding peace again in routine things, began dreaming about the girls when they were healthy, something I hadn't done for years. I looked forward to smelling my roses in the morning, digging in my vegetable garden, feeling the sun on my face, taking walks around the park at the end of the day when the air was cooling and a warm breeze would brush by. I enjoyed cooking again and sharing the outcome with my mom and friends. We started to find a new rhythm in our lives. It never would be as it was when the girls were alive, but we were on a new journey with them not by our side, but in our hearts.

The word I would use to describe it is "grateful." I began to feel grateful for the life we had had with the girls and all the love we shared, grateful that Jeff and I were still together and had found passion again, grateful for so many supportive friends and family.

My gratitude has only deepened with time. We know we will never feel the joy we felt when our daughters were here with us, but our memories hold the bond we once shared and we carry that with us always. I wrote this poem for Jeff, trying to capture my feelings at this time:

> *I always wake on Thursday morning in time to catch their last breath*
> *We thought we could protect each other*
> *We thought we could protect Charlotte and Vanessa*
> *We thought we could protect our small family against the pain*
> *But we couldn't.*
> *In the end you could only sit silently by, holding their hands*
> *Me lying next to their frail bodies,*
> *My arms wrapped tightly around them*
> *Trying to hold on to the last vestiges of their escaping breath.*
> *Talking to them, as I had promised, trying to keep them safe in their*
>   *journey*
> *So all alone.*
> *You said you hoped you had been a good dad,*
> *That you wished you could have achieved more for us to be proud of.*
> *Don't you know,*
> *You are my knight in shining armor, always to the rescue,*
> *forever there for us.*
> *The iron strength of a man wrapped softly, sweetly in tenderness.*
> *You can see by the men they chose to love and cherish,*
> *You were their stellar example.*
> *I thank you.*
> *Now we have only one another to protect, comfort, caress.*
> *I will protect you*
> *I will give you strength*

And I will love you through all of our unbearable sadness.
I have started to climb out of the deep abyss of grief,
I have reluctantly squeezed myself back into some semblance of living.
Come with me my love, we need to touch again, kiss deeply again,
Keeping the memory of their touch, their smell, their smiles alive in us.
And they will smile with us
All of us protected in this love we all still share.

A friend who lost two children to cancer years ago told me that feeling like you want to run away and hide from everyone, including your loved ones, is normal after your child dies. But, she said, then in time you realize how important it is to be with the person who went through it all with you.

That is what happened to me. No one in my life knew the pain of losing the girls more than Jeff did, living it everyday, loving the girls as much as I did. It either binds you together or tears you apart. For me it was very comforting knowing we were going through this together, sometimes having the exact same thoughts when we saw something to remind us, like the first time we went to the movies, months after Vanessa died, to see "My Dog Skip." As the movie ended and the credits rolled onto the screen, we looked at one another with tears in our eyes, and we knew what the other was thinking; the girls would have loved this movie.

Every day we keep the girls alive in our life, sharing memories and experiences that happen along the way. We have that to hold on to.

Actually, through all of this sorrow, I have never really thought "why did this happen to us?" Our sadness is in missing the girls, not why it happened, especially when we experience something beautiful or extraordinary or even ordinary. Simple things can take me to the saddest of places, but now I know it's okay because it's only temporary. I wasn't sure before.

∅ß

I was talking one day to a man I had met only five minutes before and somehow the conversation turned to the girls, probably he asked if I had children. I started to tell him about Charlotte and Vanessa when all of a sudden I was crying, which doesn't happen often in those circumstances. He looked at me and tears came to his own eyes and he told me about his brother who had died nearly twenty years ago. He had never allowed himself to grieve for him.

He finished his story with a deep sigh and told me it was first time he was able to talk about his brother since he died, and he thanked me. I now know that when these things happen there's a reason why I feel a need to share my story with a stranger.

Sometimes when a person hears about the girls, they say they couldn't have survived it. To tell you the truth, I don't know myself how Jeff and I survived. You just do. Really, if I stayed in that place of sadness, where I could go very easily, I couldn't do it, but I don't go there much. I am trying to carry on with who they were, and that gives me strength. I believe they were afraid that Jeff and I would not stay together after they died. It would make them so sad if we could not see the beauty of the world they helped us to experience again.

Chapter 56

Papa Blue, Pat

"The sadness now sits deep within me, sometimes a silent shadow, sometimes gently nudging me when I see my friends become grandmothers, families playing on the beach, kids running in the waves, everyone looking so comfortable in their skin. I can't tell what will spark it, but I allow it to surface, needing to acknowledge its presence. I accept this as me now and it is okay. It is part of loving the girls."

Pat

At this point in our lives the last thing we wanted was change, but I guess we had more to learn.

In June of 2002, Bayer spun off the division in which Jeff worked and he had a choice, move or find another job. He had traveled to Chattanooga almost every week for over two years after Vanessa died and the prospect of looking for another job was daunting. We chose to move to Chattanooga.

While packing, I found my own waist long braid I had cut years before. I hadn't been able to part with Vanessa's braid until now. I sent both braids to Stephanie and she delivered them to Locks of Love, but now there were three; she had cut her own hair the night before and included it in the gift.

ᴐᴑ

On November sixteenth, after the moving van left our empty house, we headed south, starting out early in the morning, the car packed with our most precious pictures and possessions. Leaving everyone and everything we knew behind really didn't hit me until we were driving through the Blue Ridge Mountains. Then it hit me; I was losing the girls for a second time.

At that moment, tears fell and didn't stop for days. I was cleaning our new house and crying, moving in and crying. The tears just kept coming and then they stopped. There were no more tears left.

I started thinking about The Children's Hospital of Philadelphia where I had worked as the Director of Grateful Families. There was a special day each year when we recognized gifts received in memory or in honor of a child. On the day the plaques were placed on the wall, parents came and stood in front of their child's name, silent, sometimes holding hands, many with tears in their eyes; needing to see that their child was not forgotten. I now understood.

Living far from friends and family, away from anyone who knew the girls', we wouldn't be sharing stories about them or hear their name brought up in casual conversation. I guess I wasn't ready for that.

Leaving our friends, familiar places, not being able to visit the cemetery, all these losses consumed me, but over time I grew to appreciate our home on Missionary Ridge. It became our new sanctuary, overlooking the hazy rolling mountains.

I should not have worried about leaving the girls back in Pennsylvania; they soon followed us to Chattanooga. Over the years when the girls were growing up on the farm, we saw a resurgence of bluebirds in the area and began seeing more and more nesting in the boxes we put up around the property; seeing the iridescent blue forms dart across the fields always stopped us in our tracks. When the girls died, Jeff carved their initials on two bluebird houses and placed them in a tree overlooking their graves.

Now in Chattanooga, on Vanessa's third memorial we bought a locally made bluebird house. Carved from a tree, it was round with the bark still attached, and there was a removable green metal roof one could look inside to check the babies. Jeff placed it on a tall pole in the back yard and then I asked Vanessa to send us a bluebird.

Later in the afternoon, a male bluebird sat on the roof of the house; a few minutes later a female showed up. It took some convincing to lure his mate to this house. He flew into the hole over and over again, popping his head out to look up at the female sitting in the tree. After awhile, she had enough and flew away.

While he was trying to convince her this was the right place to settle down, a pair of chickadees began setting up house, flying in and out with nesting supplies in their mouths, a nest in the making, but not for long. The following morning papa bluebird, not the chickadee, was flying in and out of house. His perseverance had paid off.

Looking in the box a few days later, we saw that there on the bottom was a neatly woven nest of dried pine straw, a classic bluebird nest; only this one had two small feathers entwined, one pale blue and one pale red, the same size but different colors, unusual for bluebirds. I felt it was the girls saying hello, and I thanked them for the gift. The blues had moved in.

Thrilled to have a pair of nesting blues so soon, I mentioned this while walking with a neighbor the next day. She said, "I've been living on the ridge for fourteen years, and I've never seen a bluebird here. You're so lucky." I doubted it was luck.

My next stop was the wild birdseed store for food to feed papa and momma. They told me that mealworms were their favorite so I bought one hundred of them.

They were right. Each morning I filled the small glass dish on the deck with the mealworms squiggling around. While mama was forming the eggs inside her belly, the two would land on the railing of the deck. Mama would then flap her wings and papa would pick up a worm from the dish and feed her. This worked fine until papa got greedy and would eat five for her one. I swear I could almost see her sneer at him when he was pigging out. But mama was smart. She began eating from the dish herself.

Looking inside the nesting box after a few weeks, I saw that there were six blue eggs. Mama now only came out to eat. They learned quickly where their food supply was and soon it was a morning, noon, and nighttime ritual. The amount they ate grew larger and larger each day, especially when the six eggs hatched.

Mama and papa followed the highway in the sky, a straight line from the deck railing to the opening in their house. Sometimes when they flew out of the nesting box for another round of worms, they would be carrying something white in their beaks. I looked in the guide to birds and found out it was the chicks' waste; they kept a very clean house. When the dish was empty, mama went off to catch bugs for her chicks, but she would pass by the dish to see if it had been replenished. If it had, she would leave the bug in the dish until she emptied it of worms and then come back for the bug. Watching their antics was my entertainment.

One morning mama was acting strange outside their house. Reaching for the binoculars, I saw a chick stick its head out of the hole. Mama and papa were atwitter, flying around and sitting on top of the house. They were obviously trying to encourage the chick to fly out. Mama came up to the deck, grabbed a worm in her beak, flew back inside the house, and came back out with the worm to entice the chick to follow.

It took awhile for the first one to finally take that leap of faith and fly, landing on the fence, teetering back and forth, trying to keep its balance and then get up the nerve to fly up into the tree where papa was squawking to get its attention. The next one came out quickly, as if it had been in line and was tired of the whole business. Watching as each one was coaxed out of the comfort of their nest, I couldn't help noticing that they looked as though they were having a bit of trouble with gravity, due to their weight. I guess I had overdone it with the mealworms. Eventually, they got the hang of flying and mama and papa were busy trying to keep track of their brood.

The day after the chicks fledged, they disappeared into the valley. This only made mama and papa's job harder because they still had to keep them fed; only it was a lot farther to go. Sometimes mama would pack up to eight squiggly worms at a time in her beak before she flew off to find her chicks. Papa, on the other hand, would leave with three worms at the most, but only after he ate more than that himself. As they flew off into the distance, I would usually see a mealworm or two falling from the sky.

About a week later there was lots of squawking outside, near the pine tree. I went out to look and saw that it was the chicks, fresh from their adventure in the valley. Mama and papa came swooping onto the deck, picked up as many worms as they could, and flew back to the tree to feed the hungry chicks. In the afternoon we heard the distinctive melodic bluebird song in the hickory tree above the deck. There were the chicks, sitting in a straight line on the branch overhead, except there were only four, not six.

We watched as mama and papa flew up and down, trying to satisfy their voracious appetites. Eventually it became too tantalizing for the chicks. One by one, they bravely, yet tentatively, flew down and plopped onto the wood railing, a graceful show it was not, but fun to watch.

All lined up in a row, flapping their gray wings, not yet the distinctive iridescent blue coloring of an adult; they opened their mouths to be fed. The preferred position was closest to the dish since that chick would be fed the most worms, which meant the most aggressive of the group usually had the fullest tummy, natural selection at work before our very eyes.

After a few weeks, mama and papa would not feed the babies anymore. In fact, they would not let them near the dish, pecking at them to keep away.

Mama was ready to lay another clutch of fertilized eggs and papa started his frantic nest building in the same house, minus the old nest, which we had removed after the chicks fledged.

This time mama laid four eggs, and three hatched. By this time, the trip to the pet store for mealworms was every few days and it was getting expensive. A friend suggested I try finding them on the Internet.

Calling Oregon after scanning hundreds of sites, I placed an order for ten thousand mealworms. After speaking to Jeff, who gasped when he heard ten thousand, I changed the order to half that amount.

They came by three-day mail, shipped in a box filled with holes. We could hear the worms moving around the shredded newspaper inside the burlap bag. When the mailman came to the door to deliver the package, he cautiously asked, "So what's in the box? It was the talk of the post office this morning. We could hear something moving." When I revealed the secret, he laughed and asked for the address to give his wife, who wanted to attract bluebirds.

Carefully going through the newspaper overflowing with fat little mealworms, I saw that they were much livelier than the ones from the pet store. I thought how the bluebirds would love these juicy little fellows. After their long journey across the country, I filled a large tray with oatmeal and some celery stalks tucked in for moisture to nourish them.

In the morning when I went get some worms for the birds' dish, I noticed that the celery stalks had been completely eaten, not a shred left, and scattered over the entire surface of the oatmeal were golden colored molted skins. Under the surface, the oatmeal was moving in waves and when it was brushed aside, the worms were twice as big as the day before. Transferring the oatmeal and about 300 worms into plastic containers, I put them into the refrigerator for hibernation so they would stop growing.

Needless to say, the bluebirds feasted happily on these plump, super-sized worms and this was an affordable way to keep my new friends satiated.

By the time the third brood started feeding from the deck, I had the system down pat. Another batch of ten thousand mealworms had just arrived in the mail, but that night at feeding time, there wasn't a bluebird in sight. Over the next few days, there was still no sign of them.

Here were ten thousand plump, juicy mealworms ready for feasting with no bluebirds to feed. Not knowing what to do, I called the wild bird store. "Oh, they're on vacation!" The woman said. "They usually leave after the chicks are on their own. They go and enjoy themselves somewhere. They probably will be back in late October or next spring to start their families again." Well, yes, I was happy for Mr. and Mrs. Blue, but what about the ten thousand mealworms sitting in my refrigerator?

I called the aquarium, where Brian the ornithologist said, "Sure we could use them. We have a standing order for thirty thousand every two weeks, but why don't you just feed them to your other birds; wrens especially like them."

We exchanged stories about our blues, since he raises them at the aquarium before they are sent to other aquariums and zoos throughout the country. When the chicks fledge in the exhibits, he has to take them out before they land on the waiting snakes and crocodiles.

I took his advice, and the Carolina wrens, chickadees, titmice and woodpeckers happily gobbled up all the worms. The small, energetic chickadees especially loved them, although it was a big task for them to wrestle down these super-sized worms.

Now, having been self-educated in the care and feeding of bluebirds, I look forward to next spring, anticipating the arrival of mama and papa blue. Thank you Vanessa and Charlotte for sending me this little family to care for.

Chapter 57

Vanessa, Pat

"In the light of world—all thoughts, there weaves the soul, who was united with me on earth."

A prayer

I had been looking for a locket for the girls' pictures ever since our trip to Petaluma with Vanessa. Not long before Mother's Day, I went to the mall with my friend Karen to buy a baby gift. I couldn't find what I was looking for and was about to leave when we passed by a jewelry store that was going out of business. Immediately I thought of Vanessa so we went inside to look around. While Karen was at the cashier buying a small cut glass lamp, I happened to see in the nearly empty case behind her a small tear-shaped gold locket; funny to notice one now when I wasn't looking anymore.

Even before the sales person removed it from the case, I knew it was the one. It opened by your sliding the front and back in opposite directions, revealing two oval picture frames, one in front and one in back, separate when open, together when closed. It was perfect. The price was $185.00. I asked how much that would be with the discount. He said $45.00. I couldn't believe it, this made me very happy.

I went home and put a very small strand of the girls' hair in each side and found the perfect picture of each of them in a photo taken on Christmas morning when they were two years old. Then I went to my jewelry box for the long gold chain I used to wear with the peace sign I had made as a teenager. The chain was just the right length. When I placed it over my head, the locket lay over my heart.

Jeff walked in from work at that moment and I told him how happy I was about my luck. But I knew it wasn't luck, it was Vanessa, leading me all the way. Even to the jewelry store to have a small, "C" and "V" engraved on either side. Thank you, Vanessa, for the treasure.

✍✎

The hellos kept coming. When Darius was ready for me to go through Vanessa's things, my sister Jan and I went over to his mom's house. While going through one of the many boxes that held her vast elephant collection, we came across a small porcelain elephant my sister had given Vanessa when she was a little girl. The gray and white elephant was only about two inches tall, including its upturned trunk, which had broken off. "Do you want this, since you gave it to Vanessa?" I asked my sister. "Sure, I'll just glue it and you won't be able to tell it was ever broken."

When we got back to her house, I unwrapped the elephant and some other treasures we had found to give to Stosh, my sister's daughter. "Jan, the tail is missing," I said as I placed the elephant on the desk. "Do you still want it?" "Yes, it must have been so small we didn't really notice it," she replied.

That was on Wednesday. On Saturday morning, my birthday, I woke up and took out things from my luggage to wear. As I unfolded a shirt, something very tiny dropped onto the window seat cushions. I looked all around until I found a sliver of something. I looked at it closely and couldn't believe what I was seeing: it was the missing elephant's tail. "What in the world was that doing in a shirt in my luggage?" was my first thought. But I stopped asking and immediately knew it was a gift from Vanessa. Her elephant could not be without its tail and it was her way of wishing me a happy birthday.

And the "hellos" continued. In December, my sister and I flew to Flagstaff, Arizona, to visit my brother, his wife and their two daughters. We visited Sedona for the day and while we were driving around town, we saw The Chapel of the Holy Cross, a small Catholic Church precipitously built between two large natural stone pillars high on a canyon wall. We parked the cars and walked up the long, steep path into a courtyard in front of the chapel. The view of the surrounding desert was spectacular. As we entered the dark chapel through the large wooden doors, we were drawn to the light streaming through the stained glass windows at the back of the altar. The sun was high in the sky and the colors were brilliantly lit from behind.

I asked my brother's daughters, Bianca and Annika, if they wanted to light a candle for Charlotte and Vanessa. We walked over to the row of candles and as I was leaning down to help them, I became aware of the hymn playing in the background, On Eagles Wings, which had been played at Charlotte's memorial. I had to sit down. As I struggled to find a tissue, the hymn ended and Amazing Grace began, the hymn we played at Vanessa's memorial. My sister and I sat next to one another until the music was over and silence filled the chapel. We looked at one another and agreed it had to be the girls saying hello.

We emerged from the cool recesses of the chapel into the bright Arizona sunshine as I called Jeff to tell him what just had happened; the girls were again saying hello. I just wish he could have been there to share the moment.

Over the years, I have been back and forth to California several times to go through Charlotte and Vanessa's things. When Caleb moved again a few years back, we were faced with the last boxes of clothes. It was very difficult after so long, but when I opened one of the suitcases, her scent filled the air; it was wonderful. For a while afterwards, I could just close my eyes and be back with Charlotte and Vanessa. Now after all these years, their scent has faded and I miss it.

Every day now, I wear Charlotte's engagement ring and the watch we gave to her at her graduation. I also wear the antique sapphire ring we bought Vanessa in fifth grade and the necklace she gave to me the day before she died.

I still wear some of their clothes, especially Vanessa's, since she was a clotheshorse. It makes me feel close to them when I am wrapped in a favorite sweater or pair of pajamas. I gave Stephanie and my friend Betsy many of Vanessa's clothes and I love when they wear them. The last time I was with Stephanie, she came out in the morning wearing a pair of Vanessa's favorite shoes. I am so grateful for moments like those.

Chapter 58

Charlotte, Jeff

"I'll be that wind that comes along and blows the trees. I believe I'll be there somewhere. Looking down on everyone, making sure they are okay."

Charlotte

After many moves and changes in our life since the girls died, we decided to again settle in Pennsylvania. It's good to be back with friends and all of our shared memories. We realize how rich our life is, and again, we are grateful.

On November eleventh, on Charlotte's memorial, we awoke to a beautiful day, a Charlotte kind of day. In the early afternoon, we drove out to the cemetery in Chester Springs bearing red roses. As we walked up the hill toward the grave, Jeff pointed up ahead, "Look, there's a bluebird." I glanced in the direction he was pointing as a mama bluebird flew close to us, but then we saw it wasn't just one bluebird, it was more than twenty. When we approached the girl's headstone, we watched in amazement as they flew all around us. We saw magnificent papa blues flying together in formation, while others were fluttering overhead and mama blues were right there with them, some even coming down to sit on the headstone. We had never seen so many bluebirds in one place.

We stayed for over an hour watching, and the blues stayed with us. They followed as we walked up the hillside to sit on the large stone bench under the tall pines overlooking the cemetery and valley. We sat for awhile just holding hands, "It's the girls, I said, they must be saying hello. I'm glad they haven't lost us in our travels." We watched the blues darting in all directions around us. "I think they're glad we're home."

Chapter 59

Lucas, Pat, Vanessa

"I'll be whispering in everyone's ear. I'll be those pesky leaves blowing off the trees; I hope to God I will be there, watching people grow and living their lives—and hopefully be happy."

Vanessa

Seven years have passed and I am again on my way to California, only this time to await a birth. Stephanie and Ian were married a year after Vanessa died. They had a special place in their wedding ceremony for Vanessa. On my birthday in 2005, they had a little boy they named Lucas. Last fall, Stephanie called to say she was pregnant again.

A few months later, in December, the phone rang. It was Stephanie calling from the doctor's office in California. She had just had her first ultrasound. "Guess what, we just found out we are having a girl and we want to name her Vanessa. Is that okay?" "Okay, are you kidding?" I replied. She started laughing. "Oh, and one more thing; she is due on your birthday." I could almost hear the girl's giggling.

This time when I stepped off the plane it felt good to be back. While I was waiting for my baggage, Ian called to say he was coming to pick me up; Stephanie was taking longer than usual at the doctor's office.

He arrived with Lucas in the back seat smiling tentatively as I leaned down to give him a kiss. While settling into my seat, Ian held up his arm and showed me a plastic hospital bracelet on his wrist. "Wow!" I said, "Times have changed. It's great they check you in at the doctor's office before the baby is born so you don't have to wait at the hospital anymore." He just looked at me and laughed. "Vanessa was born last night at 10:02. She was born on Jeff's birthday. The girls must be working overtime." He beamed as he continued the story.

"Stephanie almost didn't make it to the hospital. We arrived five minutes before she delivered. As we came through the emergency room door, they rushed her onto a stretcher and with the next contraction her water shot across the room. During the second contraction, Vanessa was born. The labor was so quick Vanessa's lungs didn't have time to push out the mucus, so she is in the ICU on a bi-pap machine, the same thing the girls were on, only its a lot smaller. It was more of a precaution and she is doing well."

"How much did she weigh?" "Six pounds eleven ounces." Charlotte had died at six eleven in the morning. It was a lot to take in all at once.

When we arrived at their house, I dropped off my bags and we drove over to the hospital to see Stephanie and Vanessa. Stephanie was all smiles and told me Vanessa had just been taken off the bi-pap and was breathing on her own. We walked over to the Intensive Care Unit to see her.

As I picked her up in my arms, I was amazed at how tiny she was, yet realized she weighed more than twice what Vanessa weighed when she was born.

When the time came that afternoon to fill out the birth certificate, they chose the name Vanessa Annabella and of course, there was a story behind it.

About a month before Vanessa was born, Stephanie, Ian and Lucas went to Muir Woods, a beautiful redwood forest on the California coast, a place the girls loved. While they were walking on a quiet trail, white butterflies flew in from all directions, surrounding them. Amidst all of them, a single orange and black butterfly with a white accent, settled on Ian's shoulder for a long time, so Stephanie took a picture of it. When they returned home and looked it up in their butterfly book, they saw that the name of the butterfly was Vanessa Annabella, or West Coast Lady. They decided then that the baby's middle name had been chosen for them.

Ian later told me that on the afternoon of Vanessa's birth, he was working in their backyard and a butterfly stayed around him for the longest time. It finally landed near his foot and he jokingly said to it, "I guess you're coming today." Later, when he went into the house, Stephanie told him she needed to get to the hospital and Vanessa was born eight days early.

∞∞

I stayed for a month to help with Vanessa, as I had with Lucas, singing nursery rhymes, reading to Lucas, changing diapers, taking walks; it felt wonderful being part of a family again.

When the day came for me to leave, I received a call that my one o'clock flight had been cancelled and that I was rescheduled on the red eye. In the afternoon while the kids were sleeping, I went out to the patio to relax for a few minutes. I noticed that a fish in the pond was stuck in the rocks, so I freed it and sat back in my chair to watch a bird fly over the fence to land in their little creek. At first I didn't pay much attention, but all of a sudden I noticed the telltale blue of a female blue-bird, only the western variety. For all the years I had spent in California, I had never seen a bluebird. Not once.

I called Stephanie and by the time she came down the steps, there were two females and two males splashing in the water. Stephanie, a native Californian, told me she had never seen a bluebird in her entire life, not in California, not anywhere.

They stayed awhile, flying between the trees in the yard and in the open field across the street. As we watched them, I somehow knew the girls would be there long after I was gone, looking after everyone. Thank you girls.

"For as long as we treasure the memories we hold
They will remain immortal and never grow cold
And when our time comes to join them above
We will pass their strength to those we love.
For if remembered well, we never die
Only spread our wings and eternally fly."

Vanessa

Afterword

I started down the path of writing "In the Morning Light" after a conversation Vanessa and I had with best selling author Mary Ann Schafer, author of *The Guernsey Literary and Potato Peel Pie Society*. She read Vanessa and Charlotte's five children's books and thought they were "wonderful", but after sending them to a colleague in the publishing business in New York, was told there was a better chance of having them published if I wrote a memoir of our story first. It has been a twelve-year journey.

Sometimes it feels like one hundred years ago and sometimes like it was yesterday, but I hope by writing this book it will give others a little insight into our life and help them in theirs.

Jeff and I presently live in Pennsylvania and find enjoyment in simple things like long walks, a ride to the shore, anything to get us out into nature. We currently are deciding what the next stage of our life will be and struggle with where to live, since our hearts are tied to the West coast, where we frequently visit.

I now move on to what I originally set out to do, keeping my promise to Charlotte and Vanessa to publish their five children's books, hoping others will experience the playfulness, inspiration and joy they found in sharing their life experiences through writing and illustrating. I know the girls' will be smiling when it happens.

Today I picked the first daffodils of spring, placing some by each of the girls' photos and a few next to my bed. As I fall asleep with the lemony fragrance all around me, I am hoping to dream of summer days long gone by.

About the Author

I have been a waitress, secretary, weaving teacher, artist, public relations assistant, senior fundraiser, caregiver, and Vice President. Nothing I have accomplished compares to being a mom and raising Charlotte and Vanessa, who continue to influence my life.

Born and raised in New Jersey, I graduated Summa Cum Laude from Rosemont College, when I was forty. I've lived in nine states and spent a year in Sweden, learning to weave, spin and dye yarn. While writing this memoir, I was awarded a six-week writing residency at the Ucross Foundation in Ucross, Wyoming.

Lucky in love, I have been married to Jeff, the love of my life, for thirty-eight years. We found one another when we were young, and although we have had such sorrow in our lives, it was entwined with laughter and joy, which has made our love grow stronger. We are grateful for the passion we still share.

I am a member of "Mother's Finding Meaning Again", a special group of mothers who have lost children. We come together once a month to give strength and hope to one another, knowing we are not alone and that sometimes understanding does not need words.

Nature is an important source of healing for me so most days I walk, volunteer, and work in my garden. I also follow a healthy diet and practice yoga. Once a week, I monitor a blue bird trail on properties not far from my home, watching the cycle of life unfold before my eyes. It brings me happiness.

PatriciaRobbins.com

Made in the USA
San Bernardino, CA
19 March 2018

An uplifting love story inspired by Charlotte and Vanessa, identical twins, their parents, and the two young men who loved the girls, all living in the shadow of cystic fibrosis. Charlotte and Vanessa followed their dreams and had full lives, facing their challenges with courage, laughter and love, leaving this Earth the way they lived, with dignity and grace.

"I caught glimpses of two young ladies who have filled their cups to the brim with love and with life. I will always remember how courageous they were—never before has a patient touched me in this way."
— Merrill Nisam, MD

"This is a tender, beautiful narrative with heart wrenching realities about a family's eternal love before and after the death of their beloved adult twin daughters to cystic fibrosis. Will especially resonate with parents of special needs children."
— Mary Jane Hurley Brant
    Author of *When Every Day Matters: A Mother's Memoir on Love, Loss and Life*

"Pulled me by my heart with words that are raw and honest and shows us that survival is possible. The affirmation that love never dies is beautifully revealed through the signs and messages sent when one might least expect them."
—Candace Apple
    Owner, Phoenix & Dragon Bookstore

Patricia Robbins, former Vice President of Hospital Development, artist, weaver, teacher, caregiver and nature lover has performed many roles in her life. The most important role will always be as mother to Charlotte and Vanessa. They were her teachers and filled her life with joy.

PatriciaRobbins.com

It is not how many pages your life story holds, but what is written within.

$12.95
ISBN 978-0-578-10813-1
51295>

9 780578 108131